ZULU

To our parents with love and thanks
ROGER AND PAT DE LA HARPE

To my family and the people of South Africa
SUE DERWENT

To my mother for her wisdom and humanity, and to
Kofi Sikhakhane for the flame he lit in me
BARRY LEITCH

ZULU

PHOTOGRAPHERS: ROGER AND PAT DE LA HARPE
AUTHOR: SUE DERWENT
CONSULTANT AUTHOR: BARRY LEITCH

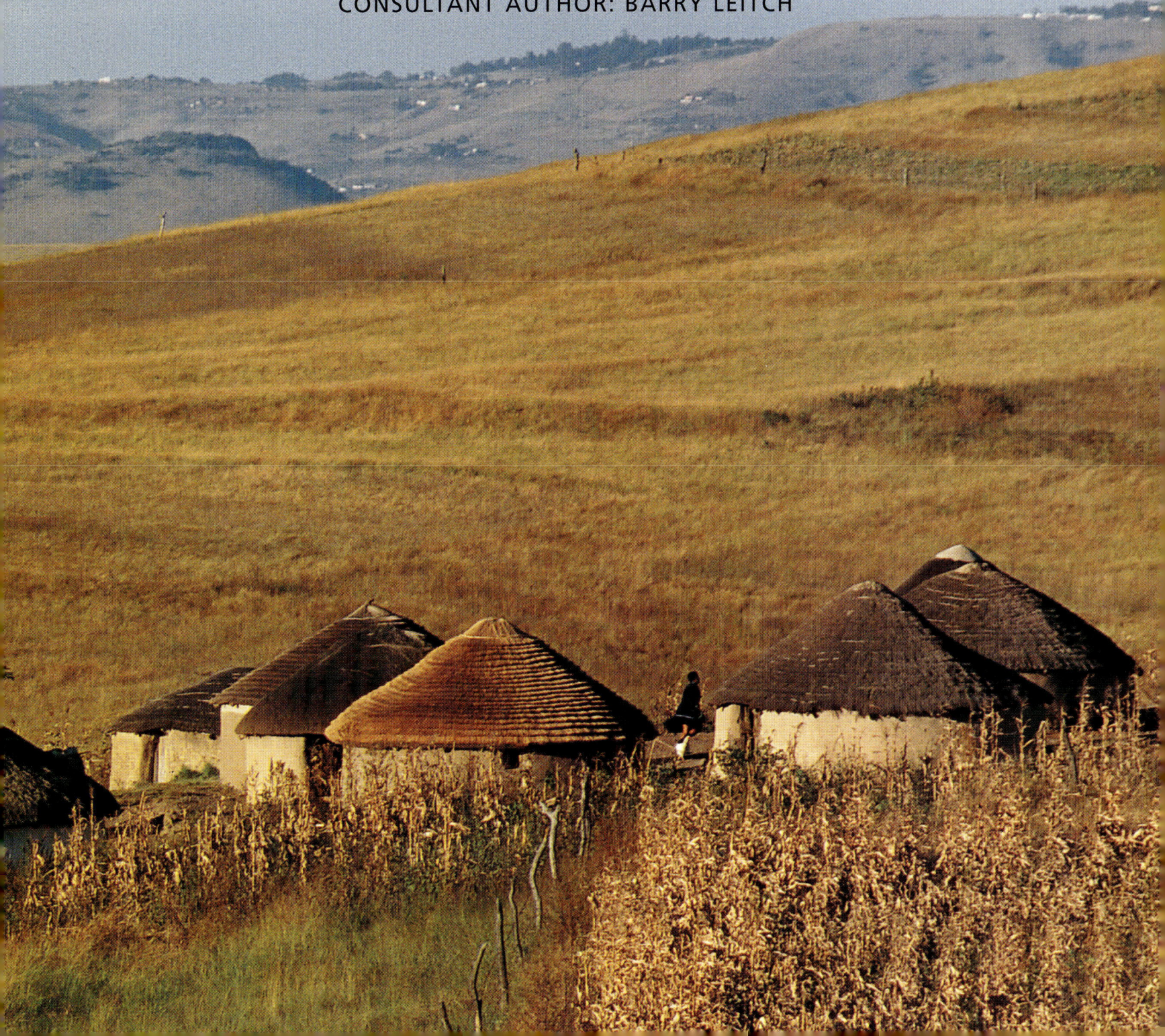

First published in 1998 by Struik Publishers (Pty) Ltd
(A member of Struik New Holland Publishing (Pty) Ltd)
London • Cape Town • Sydney • Singapore
Registration number 54/00965/07

80 McKenzie Street   24 Nutford Place   3/2 Aquatic Driver
Cape Town 8001   London W1H 6DQ   Frenchs Forest, NSW
South Africa   United Kingdom   2086 Australia

ISBN 1 86872 082 9

10 9 8 7 6 5 4 3 2 1

Managing editor: Annlerie van Rooyen
Designer: Janice Evans
Editor: Lesley Hay-Whitton
Design assistants: Sonia Hedenskog-de Villiers and Lellyn Creamer
Cartographers: Desiree Oosterberg and Mark Seabrook
Consultant: Dr. Sandra Klopper
Indexer: Brenda Brickman
Proofreaders: Annelene van der Merwe and Cliff Dikeni

Reproduction by Hirt & Carter Cape (Pty) Ltd
Printed and bound by Tien Wah Press (Pte.) Ltd, Singapore

PAGE 1: *The position of Zulu men is increasingly being threatened by
the empowerment of women.*
PAGES 2 AND 3: *A typical Zulu homestead (umuzi) in rural KwaZulu-Natal.*
PAGES 4 AND 5: *The job of looking after the family's herd of cattle
traditionally falls to the boys' lot.*

ACKNOWLEDGEMENTS

Thanks to the patriarchs Gilenja Biyela, Golozela and John
Sikhakhane who are but a few of the Zulu people in whose shadows
we grew up and who taught us to love the Zulu ethos, with its deep-
seated humanity (*uBuntu*) which underpins many of the colourful
Zulu traditions that are enshrined in this book.   BARRY LEITCH

We wish to thank Kodak South Africa for its sponsorship and in
particular Peter Milton and Grant Bester for their assistance and
support. Our appreciation to Max Fowles and his staff at CityLab
(Durban) for their sponsorship and care taken in processing our
film. A special thanks to François Meyer, Joanne Deall and staff at
Shakaland, and Vanessa and Alex Leitch and staff at Simunye Zulu
Lodge for their hospitality and assistance. Our thanks, too, for
their endless patience and help, to Vincent Sikhakhane, Lungani
Ndlovu, Blessing Dube, Sue Duffus, Julianne Calitz and Victor
(2 Bullet) Zakwe. To the Struik team, in particular Janice Evans,
Annlerie van Rooyen and Lesley Hay-Whitton, our thanks. Finally,
to Barry Leitch and Sue Derwent, it was a pleasure working with
you.   ROGER AND PAT DE LA HARPE

I wish to thank the staff at Simunye and shakaland, Barry Leitch
and his family, and the Struik team.   SUE DERWENT

PLEASE NOTE: Wherever possible, we have attempted
to name the people depicted in this book
THE PUBLISHERS.

CONTENTS

PREFACE

In the months that it took us to put together a book on the Zulu, all four of us, Pat and Roger de la Harpe, Barry Leitch and I, have all learned an enormous amount, and not just about putting a book together. Working with the Zulu people, who opened their hearts and their lives to us and who welcomed us into their homes, has expanded our concept of not only the Zulu people themselves, but of our country and our selves.

Many books have been written about the Zulu people, but mostly from a political or historical point of view. When we embarked upon this project, we all understood that none of us wanted to go that route. Having spent our lives in KwaZulu-Natal – Pat and Roger having moved here from the former Transvaal a number of years ago, and Barry and I having been born in the area – we are in constant contact with Zulu people. All of us have worked or lived in rural KwaZulu-Natal over the years and, because of this, we wanted to communicate and share our experiences of ordinary Zulu people and their daily lives, with others: Pat and Roger from a visual point of view, and Barry and I as story-tellers.

It is far from easy to record a culture since no culture remains static for long. What makes it even more difficult is the fact that, as white South Africans, our credibility as analysts or interpreters of Zulu culture brings its own set of problems. However, we were fortunate to have been assisted by a wonderful group of Zulu people, without whom this book would have been impossible. Most of these people either worked or lived in and around Shakaland and Simunye, two cultural villages that were established in rural KwaZulu-Natal by Barry Leitch and his colleagues. The Zulu people involved with these villages, in the warm-hearted way of rural Zulu people, helped us enormously, not just with information of a social or historical nature, but giving of their precious time. They invited us to parties and to any number of community celebrations and special occasions so that we could 'absorb' the culture and meet the ordinary rural Zulu people and communities, whom, as white outsiders, we may have otherwise had some difficulty accessing. We attended family weddings far off in the rural areas where there are no roads and where little has changed in the last two hundred years. We were taken to coming of age ceremonies, special traditional healers' graduation ceremonies, to church services and into Zulu homes to meet grandmothers, grandfathers and other family members and share meals. We attended cattle auctions, had access to *ilobolo* (bride wealth) negotiations and were taken by a group of young people down to the river so that we could catch a glimpse of the age-old courtship rituals.

PREVIOUS PAGES: Unmarried Zulu maidens (amatshitshi) go bare-breasted and bare-headed. Once engaged, they will wear a brassière and a head-covering at weddings and coming of age and other ceremonies.

RIGHT: The early morning sun casts intriguing shadows on the mud walls of a rural house.

OPPOSITE: Many Zulu children living in rural areas are forced by economic circumstances to make their own toys, such as this wire car with its working steering.

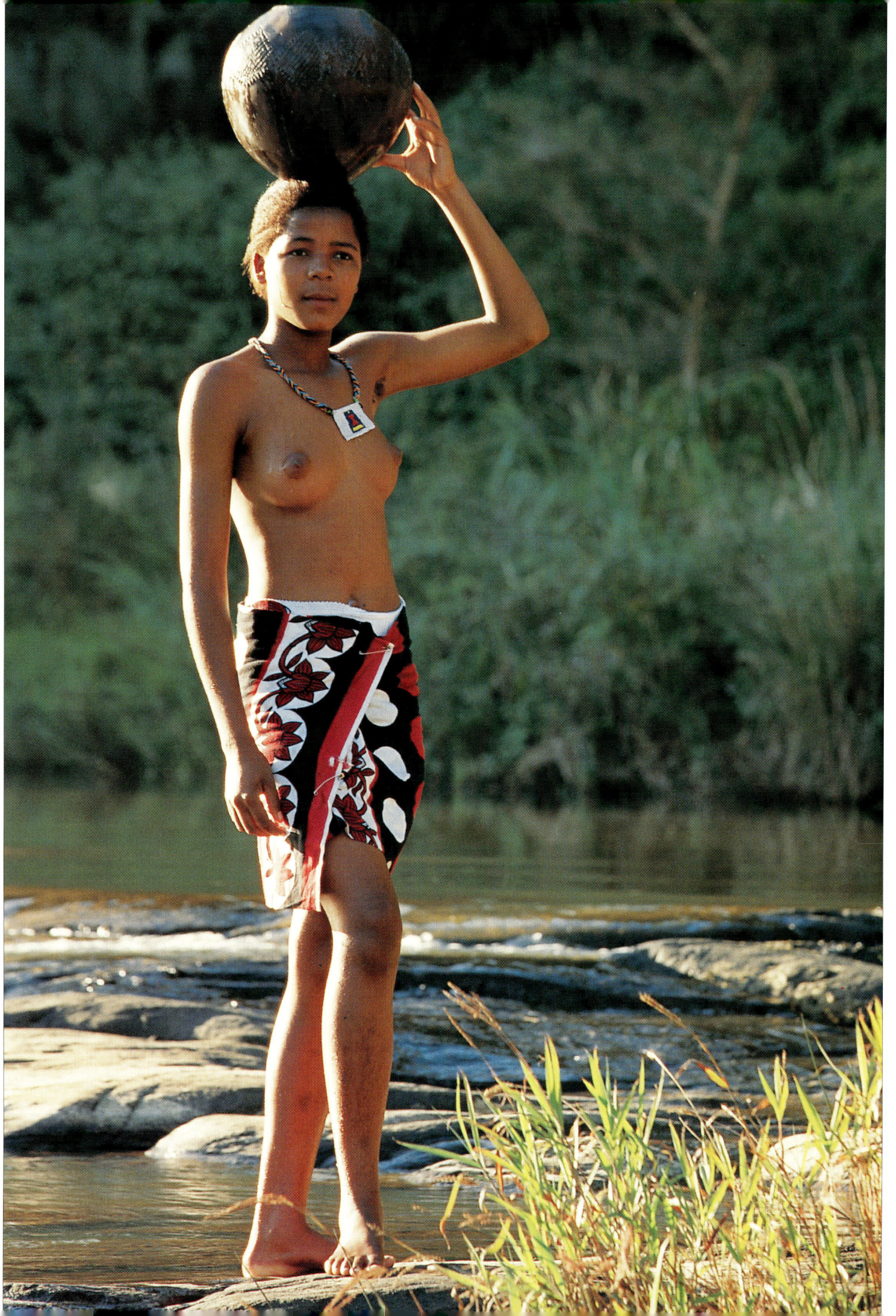

The ever-obliging staff of both Shakaland and Simunye showed us how Zulu pots, beer, spears and shields were traditionally made. Arts and crafts can be seen in their purest form in the remote areas of KwaZulu-Natal or at many of the cultural villages, but these days many of the traditional arts and crafts are practised largely for the tourist trade and are on sale in urban centres.

Throughout KwaZulu-Natal, there are variations in the interpretations of cultural activities and events. Each group of Zulu-speaking people has their own story to tell and their own way of telling it. So we were indeed fortunate in that Barry has had a life-long relationship with some of the senior members of a lineage that has played a significant role in Zulu history through the ages, the Biyela lineage, particularly the Yanguye and Obuka authorities who are located in the vicinity of the White Mfolozi River, between Melmoth and Empangeni. Barry has had a close personal relationship with Prince Gilenja, the Biyela patriarch, who accepted him as one of his honorary sons at an early age. Barry's relationship to many of the elders of this group meant that the information he has gleaned and lessons he has learned from the Zulu over the years brought an added dimension to our understanding of Zulu culture and to many of the variations. The elders of the Biyela lineage are also perhaps some of the last repositories of Zulu oral history, and we were indeed privileged to have had the opportunity to meet and talk with some of them.

It was also exciting to meet men and women who are the grandchildren and great-grandchildren of the Zulu men and women who played significant roles in Zulu history. Many of these people, though they may not be well known outside rural KwaZulu-Natal, are the descendants of famous mothers of chiefs, warrior generals and craftsmen to kings.

We hope that through this book, in some small way, we are able to show what the ordinary Zulu people mean to us, and to share our experience of their spirit which they so generously shared with us.

SUE DERWENT
BARRY LEITCH
ROGER DE LA HARPE
PAT DE LA HARPE
1998

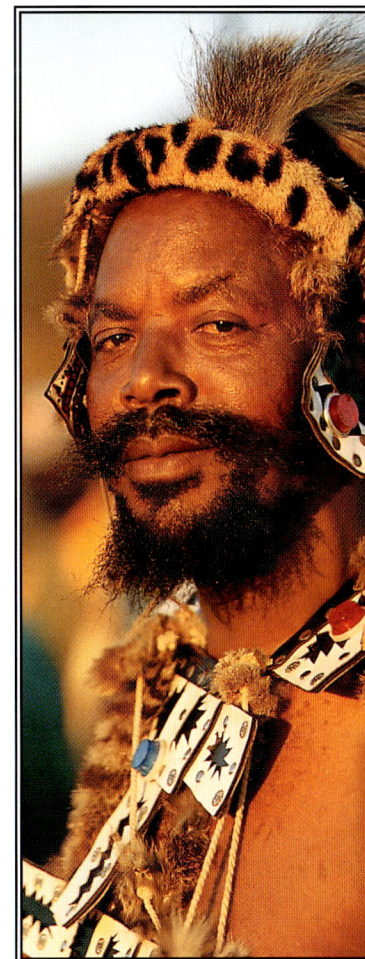

OPPOSITE: *Women in rural areas frequently have to carry clay pots full of water for long distances from the river to their homes. Traditionally women bear heavy loads in this way: on their heads.*
ABOVE: *A Zulu man decked out in his ceremonial dress. These days, elements such as bicycle reflectors are combined with the more traditional leopard skin.*
FOLLOWING PAGE: *A Zulu* umuzi *(homestead) with its traditional beehive houses nestles on the hills of rural KwaZulu-Natal.*

MAPUTO

MOZAMBIQUE

SWAZILAND

LEBOMBO

Mbabane

Hendrina

Bethal

Ermelo

Mpumalanga

Piet Retief

Standerton

Vaal

Volksrust

Charlestown

Groenvlei

Grootspruit

Commondale

Berbice

Ponta do Ouro

Kosi Bay

NDUMO
GR

TEMBE
ELEPHANT
PARK

Kosimeer

KOSI BAY NR

Ingwavuma

Lavumisa

Phongolo

Lake Sibaya

Paulpietersburg

Bivane

ITALA
GR

Pongola

Louwsburg

Pongolapoort Dam

Jozini

Sodwana Bay

Free
State

Ingogo

Utrecht

Bivane

Vryheid

Historical
Zululand

Mkuze

Ubombo

Mkuze

MKUZI
GR

Newcastle

Madadeni

Osizweni

Nongoma

PHINDA RESOURCE RESERVE

GREATER
ST LUCIA
WETLAND PARK

CHELMSFORD PUBLIC
RESORT NR

Dannhauser

Kingsley

Bloedrivier

Hluhluwe
Dam

Hluhluwe

Harrismith

Fort
Mistake

Hattingspruit

Dundee

Blood River

Where Prince
Imperial died

Black Mfolozi

Mahlabatini

Lake St Lucia

STERKFONTEIN
NR

BIGGARSBERG

Glencoe

Battle
of Talana

Blood

Nqutu

White Mfolozi

Ulundi

HLUHLUWE-
UMFOLOZI
PARK

Mtubatuba

St Lucia Estuary

Van Reenen

Wasbank

Vant's
Drift

Rorke's Drift

Babanango

Ulundi

Ondini

RUGGED
GLEN NR

Gelukburg

Elandslaagte

Rorke's
Drift

Isandlwana

eMgungundlovu

Riverview

Ladysmith

Wagon Hill

Pomeroy

Dingane's
Homestead

Piet Retief's Grave

KwaMbonambi

ROYAL
NATAL NP

Woodstock Dam

SPIOENKOP
DAM NR

Roosboom

Melmoth

DUKUDUKU
FOREST
RESERVE

Bergville

Blackhouse

Colenso

Battle of
Colenso

KwaZulu-Natal

Ndundulu

Simunye
Traditional Village

Mtubatuba

Winterton

WEENEN
NR

Tugela Ferry

Nkwalini

Empangeni

Umsingazi Lake

Frere

Bloukrans
Monument

Weenen

Kranskop

Cetshwayo's Grave

Shakaland
Traditional
Village

Site of Shaka's Homestead

Richards Bay

WAGENDRIFT
NR

Estcourt

Greytown

HINZA
FOREST
RESERVE

Coward's Bush
Monument

RICHARDS BAY NR

Fort
Mtombeni

Eshowe

Fort
KwaMondi

Felixton

UMLALAZI NR

Mooirivier

Craigieburn
Dam

Nongqai Fort

aMatikulu

Gingindlovu

NATAL
DRAKENSBERG
PARK

Rosetta

Rietvlei

New
Hanover

Dalton

Umvoti

Mandini

Fort Pearson

LESOTHO

Nottingham
Road

ALBERT
FALLS
NR

Mpolweni

Darnall

Tugela

Ultimatum Tree

Howick

MIDMAR
DAM NR

Howick
Falls

QUEEN
ELIZABETH PARK

Ndwedwe

Stanger

Shaka's Memorial

HIMEVILLE
NR

Edendale

PIETERMARITZBURG

Tongaat

Shakaskraal

Thornville

Camperdown

Inanda

Verulam

COLEFORD
NR

Underberg

Mpumalanga

Clermont

KwaMashu

DURBAN

Donnybrook

Richmond

Pinetown

Eastern
Cape

Ixopo

Umkomaas

Queensburgh

Umlazi

Isipingo

Amanzimtoti

Franklin

VERNON
CROOKES NR

Kingsburgh

Cedarville

uMzinto

MOUNT
CURRIE NR

Harding

Kelso

Kokstad

Brooks
Nek

ORIBI
GORGE
NR

Marburg

INDIAN
OCEAN

Mount Ayliff

Umtamvuna

Port Shepstone

Mount Frere

UMTAMVUNA
NR

Port Edward

Eastern
Cape

MKAMBATI NR

N

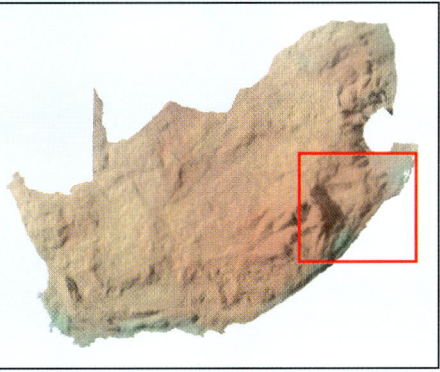

0   10 km

0   6 miles

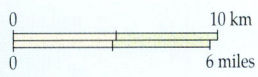

INTRODUCTION

Uzalo luhamba phambili
Blood is thicker than water

The Zulu emerged as a regional power in the early 1800s, as the legendary King Shaka began to dominate the sub-continent. In 1879 the Zulu armies inflicted a massive defeat upon the British at Isandlwana that was unprecedented in Britain's colonial history at the time. By the end of the nineteenth century the Zulu name resounded around the Western world, as the Zulu kindled people's imagination.

RIGHT: Proud of their past glory, Zulu men identify strongly with their warrior heritage.
OPPOSITE: Goboti, also known as Gumede Dludla, is a leader and warrior captain in his area. Also an excellent dancer, he leads the dancers at Shakaland. Around his neck he wears a duiker horn to carry medicines. Goboti is a spear maker by profession, one of the few still able to make the stabbing spear introduced by Shaka.

To many nineteenth-century European people, the Zulu epitomized the Romantic notion of the 'noble savage'. While they may indeed have been noble, they were far from savages. Their warfare was characterized by iron-willed discipline, and their society by a sophisticated culture, influenced by the natural environment in which they lived. In the course of the twentieth century, pride in the heritage of Zulu-speakers has been actively promoted through the first and second Inkatha movements in the 1920s and 1975 respectively. Certain traditions, such as the royal practice of wearing crane feathers, have been revived, while others, for instance the Reed Ceremony, have been introduced. Contemporary Zulu culture is full of praise poetry, idioms and values which are drawn from both natural and historic events, which characterize the Zulu people.

Astonishingly, in spite of the fact that modernization and the increasing relevance of the cash economy have invaded and altered much of Zulu life, some bastions remain unchanged; it is from these bastions that contemporary Zulu culture draws its strength. Despite numerous onslaughts, certain rituals and ceremonies have survived largely intact to this day, continuing to inform Zulu culture. These

customs are the basis of many rites of passage through which the Zulu pass in the course their lives. With the passage of time the Zulu were forced by everyday experiences in the often harsh and unpredictable environment of southern Africa, to learn from the natural world around them . . . or perish. Even though most Zulu people have, to a varying extent, become Westernized, many of them nevertheless loyally adhere to their traditional customs, rituals and ceremonies.

THE WARRIOR NATION

The Zulu are descendants of a mighty nation which was forged on military strength, and as such the warrior ethic is still alive and flourishing. This is evident in the military overlay to Zulu society witnessed not only in day-to-day dealings with proud Zulu men, many of whom still identify strongly with their glorious military past, but also in a number of other traditional Zulu ceremonies. In a Zulu dance, the men re-enact military manoeuvres and victorious battles in their dance steps; at a traditional Zulu wedding, the regiments of young men arrive singing war anthems, before breaking away to take

part in stick-fighting challenges. A group of angry, urban Zulu people, organized into their regiments, marching through the city streets singing their war-cries during a protest march, gives one a glimpse of how a large sector of the Zulu population still perceives and values their glorious heritage. Shaka's legacy to the Zulu nation was not merely the introduction into Zulu warfare of the short stabbing spear – with which he is so strongly associated. Nor was it only the forging of a highly structured and organized social hierarchy. Rather, Shaka left the Zulu with a strong sense of their position as a well-disciplined, courageous and conquering nation which, at that time more than any other, set them apart from different groupings.

THE RURAL PEOPLE

Despite all the warrior imagery that is still present in Zulu society, one of the most outstanding characteristics of the Zulu people is their heartfelt affability and humanity. It is the ordinary people who are the Zulu nation's greatest characters and its greatest ambassadors: the people living their lives in the warm hills of rural KwaZulu-Natal, playing, going to school, courting, marrying, having children, working their fields, tending their cattle, struggling and laughing; people such as feisty grandmothers who plant a patch of chillies to sell and eke out an existence.

Old people have always been held in high esteem in Zulu culture. In the past, they were revered and respected for their experience and the wisdom of their years, and more recently, perhaps, because of the broader role they have played in sustaining and holding together a culture during a difficult time in its history.

Migrant labour had become a fact of life by the mid-twentieth century, especially for the Zulu. Men had to go away to work on the mines or in the cities, and some mothers entered domestic service in the urban centres, and were unable to take their children with them. More recently, during the years of violence and fighting between the predominantly Zulu-based political organization, the Inkatha Freedom Party (IFP) (which succeeded the Inkatha Cultural Liberation Organisation founded by Buthelezi in 1975), and the African National Congress (ANC), many urban Zulu parents sent their children 'back home' to the comparatively safe rural areas. Here they could live with relatives, away from the violence in the cities. In all of these cases the children have been cared for by their grandmothers, who were, and often still are, single-handedly responsible for feeding, clothing, housing and sending their grandchildren to school. Grandmothers, who receive pensions, are frequently the main source of income in rural areas. As a result they have become increasingly powerful in the past few decades.

ZULU WOMEN

The humanity and courage of ordinary Zulu people is also epitomized by the young wife, whose husband spends most of the year away working in the city. On a tiny income she has to try to educate and feed a family in a demanding rural environment, often supported only by an elderly grandmother. The stoical good humour with which such women face the harsh challenges of life characterizes the lives of many Zulu people. Even though Zulu men may indulge in other liaisons when away from home, wives are expected to remain faithful to their men, and hold the family together. Raising children has always been the responsibility of the women. They often have to undertake rough manual labour growing crops to sustain their families. Even the tending of

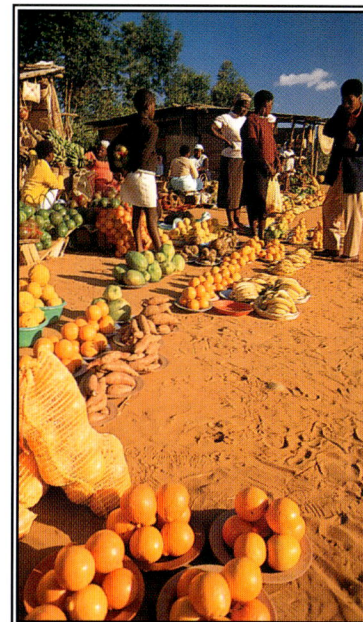

OPPOSITE: Zulu women of all ages have played a significant role in maintaining traditions and customs throughout many of the most difficult periods in their history as a nation.
ABOVE: Traditional Zulu crafts, such as pottery and baskets, are sold at numerous roadside stalls in northern KwaZulu-Natal.
FOLLOWING PAGES: Malinga, an elder, presides over Zulu male dancing, wearing his leopard skin. Malinga, who is a master craftsman, is a maker of the umncedo, *a cover made from dried strelitzia leaves that is worn over the tip of the penis. Sigonyela Ndlovu, an excellent drummer and respected member of his community because of his old-order lifestyle, heads the group of dancers as they act out many of the manoeuvres of past victorious battles.*

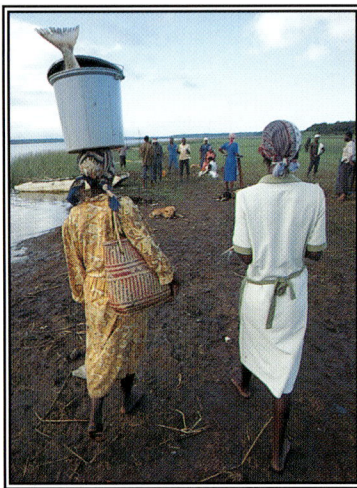

TOP: A young Zulu woman cuts Qube grass to make sleeping mats. Harvesting raw materials such as reeds and grass for building materials and household utensils can take up much of a rural Zulu woman's day.
ABOVE: A woman carrying fish caught in Lake St Lucia in the Greater St Lucia Wetland Park.

livestock, traditionally a male occupation, becomes the women's responsibility, in the absence of their men. In rural communities, which frequently do not have electricity and running water, firewood and water have to be carried for miles.

Increasingly, women are forced by economic circumstances to find work in the cities and, since the breakdown of influx controls in the late 1980s, they have been more able to do so. Often they cannot afford, or even find, accommodation for themselves, let alone for their children, in urban areas. As a result, Zulu women are often separated for extended periods, not only from their husbands who may work in a different city, but also from their children. Yet many of these women face life with a glowing and vibrant optimism that is truly inspirational. Perhaps ironically, it is through the challenge of these hardships that Zulu women have risen above their predicaments and become the indomitable people they are today.

Zulu women, both young and old, have played a significant role in keeping the fabric of Zulu society intact over the years, although this may not be the case for much longer. With better access to education and as they become more economically independent, many women are starting to challenge the fiercely patriarchal rules of Zulu society. Yet, in spite of this, culture and tradition continue to have a strong hold in rural KwaZulu-Natal, which often spills over into the urban environment. Even liberated women may find themselves hard pressed to show a total disregard for their heritage, acknowledging the solid social values it incorporates.

ZULU MEN

For Zulu men, modern cultural circumstances have also been challenging. In the past, the cream of Zulu manhood formed the elite warrior regiments, undertaking strenuous mental and physical hardship, training as warriors, and later travelling across harsh terrain for months on end, in extreme weather conditions, to fight their enemies, protect their families and conquer new territories. In those days, they were rewarded for their strength and valour with cattle, which in turn sustained the Zulu home economies. Today, the situation is very different: the battle is no longer fought in the hills of northern KwaZulu-Natal, but in the urban job market, where the rules are very different from those which prevailed on a nineteenth-century battlefield. At that time, the test of a man was his physical strength and courage, and his mental discipline in the face of adversity. He was valued for his stoicism, bravery, and ability to deal with pain and hardship in a positive manner, and for his disdain for negativity in any form. His training began, however informally, as a small boy herding cattle in the African bush, and playing at stick-fighting with his older brothers.

The 'warrior-test' of a contemporary Zulu man is to survive in an alien environment, to which he has often had little prior exposure. To a young man from a humble rural background, the traditional training which he received as a boy may not seem to have equipped him very well to deal with the daunting task of becoming a successful migrant worker and providing for his extended family back home. But, in fact, certain elements of his heritage, such as stoicism and good humour, stand him in good stead, giving him the strength needed to undertake the task.

The Zulu were forced into the cash economy as recently as 1906, when the Bambata rebellion took place at Nkandla in Zululand in reaction to the introduction of a poll tax. The British imposed this tax in an attempt to balance their budget following the post-Boer War recession. As the cash economy became increasingly prevalent in Zulu culture, it slowly began to undermine the fierce pride and independence of the old

Zulu era. In the past, a man was defined by agrarian activities, such as the ability to plough, his skills as a hunter or stick-fighter, his competency as a father and proficiency to forage and protect his family; however, with the introduction of the cash economy the rules have changed, and nowadays a man is defined by his ability to make money.

In traditional Zulu culture, power is either ascribed by birth, or a man is elected, sometimes unwillingly, into a position of leadership by his peers. For instance, warrior captains are respected men in their communities even today, because of their ability to control groups of fiery young men. They are often called upon to adjudicate at stick-fighting bouts at weddings, and these days, as in the past, during violent clashes between warring groups of neighbours or political opponents. A warrior captain is not simply appointed by the chief as one might expect. When a man is recognized for his character, his ability to earn the respect of his peers, and his general authoritative demeanour, he is thrust into a leadership role as a warrior captain by the community.

BELOW: A platoon of men, decked out in ceremonial gear. The sticks that they are carrying are ornate fighting sticks rather than those used for everyday stick-fighting.

As has already been mentioned, many Zulu men spend most of their lives in the city, and are able to go home only at Christmas and Easter. But it is usually only by making this sacrifice that they are able to sustain a traditional home life back in a rural area. Because of their homesickness and nostalgia while they are separated from their families, when they do return home, Zulu men are often the strictest proponents of upholding and maintaining the 'old Zulu order'.

The irony is that the effects of urban life which are undermining traditional Zulu culture may at the same time be playing an important part in sustaining and maintaining it. Although young Zulu men in cities are faced daily with an incredible barrage of choices and influences that fly in the face of their cultural heritage, for the most part they live an insular urban existence. Despite this, they have managed, in many ways, to impact upon their urban environment. Men living in the migrant labour hostels in the cities and towns where they work often establish 'home-boy' groups, which are small sub-communities of men from a common home territory or geographical area. These groups are usually the cutting edge of Zulu cultural activity away from home. Many of the finest contemporary Zulu dances are choreographed and executed in the incongruous setting of an urban hostel, and the same is true of music, arts and crafts. The dancing, singing and other performances by Zulu migrant workers have, to a large extent, served to reinforce their culture, and given rise to cross-pollination, as Zulu men compete with those from other Zulu 'home-boy' groups, as well as with those from different ethnic groups.

When Zulu men go home at Easter and Christmas, excitement resonates across all the territories in anticipation of the new dancing performances which they bring back from the city. The awareness of having all the men at home gives these festival times a tangible energy. Oxen are put up as prizes for the best dances, many of which reflect influences of people and different groups from regions throughout the country.

ZULU CHILDREN

Zulu children who are brought up in a traditional environment are generally well behaved. Girls are permitted to be tomboys when they are little, fighting and playing with the boys their own age; they may even stick-fight better than their brothers. However, as soon as they start growing up, they are taught to *hlonipha* elder relatives, and more especially men. This involves behaving in a respectful, even subservient, manner towards male figures of authority, for instance never allowing one's head to be on a higher level than that of a senior person. A woman will change her body language when she addresses her elders. To *hlonipha* is to affirm another person's status, and, consequently, that person's sense of self. Small boys are also taught to respect their elders, but the custom of *hlonipha* affects females more than males.

All children of both sexes are expected to undertake chores and contribute to the running of a homestead. But this does not mean that they do not have time for a carefree existence, playing in the rivers, making up games and learning to stick-fight. The lives of Zulu children have undergone a radical change in more modern times, since they have been required to attend official government schools. Despite this, many of them still continue to carry out their traditional household chores on a daily basis. Having children who can read and write around the house has resulted in a fundamental change to the dynamics of rural Zulu families. Illiterate adults, many of whom speak only Zulu, and who in the past were the ultimate voice of authority, now often have to rely on their children to translate and explain things to them.

OPPOSITE: In rural areas, young Zulu mothers continue to breast-feed their babies for extended periods, a practice not always possible for urban working women these days.
BELOW: A young boy enjoys the early morning sun before setting off to herd his father's cattle.
BOTTOM: Toddlers often have to be left in the care of only slightly older brothers and sisters while their parents are out working.

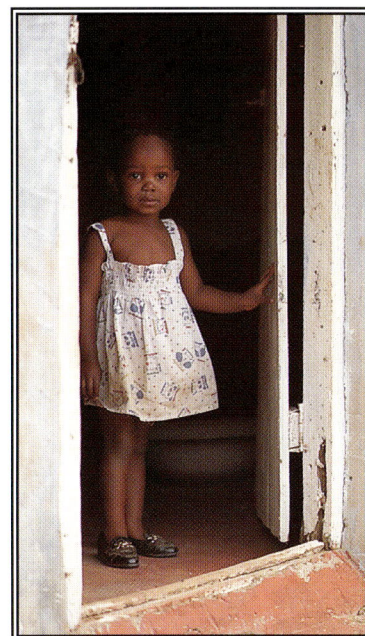

ABOVE: A Zulu community sit listening to their chief. They all sit lower than the chief out of respect for his status, a form of hlonipha.

THE COMMUNALITY OF ZULU SOCIETY

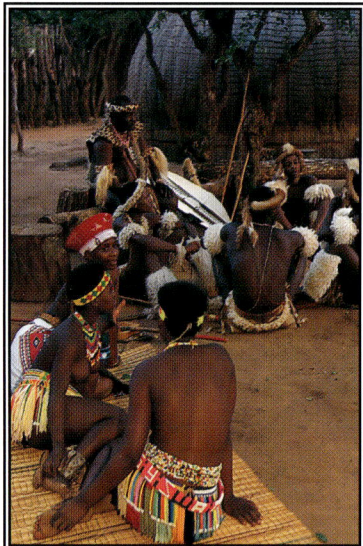

In Zulu culture, the whole is more important than the parts, and the community is more important than the individual. This leads to a paradigm quite different from the Western norm: Zulu people tend to do things for the good of society as a whole. For example, a group of brothers may pool their finances over a period of years in order to assist one of the brothers to pay for the *ilobolo* cattle (today this tends to be the cash equivalent of the cattle), the traditional bride wealth, so that he can marry. There will be no account kept of how much each person has paid into the pool; each contributes what he can. Once one brother is married, all the young men will again pool their resources in order to assist the next brother. These days, this type of communality also takes the form of assisting family members through school. Once children in the family have completed their education and are working, they in turn will help their brothers and sisters obtain an education. If one of the sisters marries, her husband or someone in her new family may also contribute towards her family's education. In this way, there is a genuine sense of sharing and an understanding that a well-educated child, or a brother happily married, can contribute to the community.

Similarly, the land and the abundance of nature belong to everyone, and are for the benefit of all. This dates back to the time when people first settled in the area that later became known as Zululand (now part of KwaZulu-Natal). The use of natural resources was usually administered by a local chief, and later by the kings and their appointed *izinduna* (headmen). Healers underwent strict training in the ethics and taboos of how plants were allowed to be harvested, and how animals should be caught and killed. In many areas, hunters had first to obtain permission from their chiefs to hunt, and certain animals could be hunted only in specific areas and at certain times of the year.

THE PAST

Many Zulu traditionalists have a historic perspective that extends far into the past. The praise poems and songs which are sung at every family wedding or ceremony reinforce, in the minds of the community, events of historic importance that go back generations. On the other hand, Zulu people often have a limited horizon stretching into the future, because for many of them it is perfectly acceptable to acknowledge that one cannot know what will happen in the future. Traditionally, it is important to be acquainted with the past and to learn from past experience and information. This attitude to the past may also explain why in Zulu society old people are always so revered. Fundamental to Zulu culture is the belief that the older you get the more important you become; therefore old people remain an important part of society, unlike in Western culture. The conviction that the past is more important than the future goes hand in hand with the belief that if you take care of your past, making sure that the all-seeing, all-knowing ancestors are not angry, and that wrong-doings are atoned for, the future will take care of itself.

THE FUTURE

Over the centuries, Zulu culture has come under enormous pressure, both internal and external, and this has caused it to change. Today there are still powerful external influences at work on Zulu culture, but much of the stress and tension of this current,

often violent, transitional period of Zulu history is being tempered by many of the underpinnings of old Zulu culture – such as the humanity, resilience and plain optimism of Zulu people. These are people who have accepted hardships and remained stoical; rural people who may not always like or understand many of the cultural changes which they are being forced to address, but who none the less for the most part accept the humanity of other people. The Zulu idiom 'uMuntu nguMuntu ngaBantu' is difficult to translate literally, but its general meaning is 'A person is only a person because of what he means to other people'; this may be said to represent the way of thinking of ordinary Zulu people. When travellers encounter a Zulu person for the first time, even though they may not speak the same language or be of the same culture, the travellers will sense that, to the Zulu person, they are fellow members of the human race, and because of that they are not strangers.

BELOW: *Local fishermen eke out a living on Lake St Lucia in the Greater St Lucia Wetland Park.*

HISTORY

Tales recounted

The independent Zulu kingdom, influential as it was, existed for a very short time: it came to power in the 1820s and was crushed in the Anglo-Zulu war of 1879. But it had repercussions far into this century. Many of South Africa's six million Zulu-speakers are still influenced by the ethos of the Zulu military system. This is especially true of migrant labourers, most of whom remain true to their rural roots, even though they spend much of their adult lives in urban centres.

RIGHT: *A lithograph vignette from Nathaniel Isaacs's* Travels and Adventures in Eastern Africa *(1836) of Shaka, who forged the mighty Zulu nation.*
OPPOSITE: *A cross near Nqutu in KwaZulu-Natal marks the grave of a British soldier who fell in the battle of Isandlwana, 1879. There are many such graves nearby.*

Large parts of the area that is now known as KwaZulu-Natal were conquered by the first Zulu king, Shaka, at the start of the nineteenth century. The early history of this region has been passed down by word of mouth through the centuries, but it was only after the arrival at Port Natal of European traders and colonists that historic events were recorded in writing. In modern times this has resulted in an uncomfortable situation: recorded by members of other cultures, Zulu history has frequently been subjected to agendas that are clearly at odds with the values and perceptions of the Zulu-speakers themselves. In recent years, however, scholars have begun to reassess and reinterpret Zulu oral tradition, in an attempt to give a less biased view of important historical events.

Zulu oral tradition tells of how Malandela, who is sometimes characterized as the father of the Zulu people, settled during the late sixteenth century on the southern banks of the Umhlatuze River, just before it enters the fertile Nkwalini Valley. At the homestead which he established at the foot of Amandawe Hill, Malandela is said to have raised his two quarrelsome sons, Qwabe and Zulu. To prevent them from fighting, Malandela later sent them to different areas to settle and build their own chiefdoms.

By the late eighteenth century, both of the chiefdoms established by the brothers paid allegiance to Dingiswayo of the Mthethwa, the most powerful leader in the region. Dingiswayo built up an army and systematically conquered and absorbed some of the small-scale political units in the area, in an apparent effort to control the region's access to trade goods like beads and cloth, and possibly also to manage scarce natural resources, such as grazing. Until the 1820s, when traders from Port Natal first made contact with Shaka, all imported prestige items were procured from the Portuguese at Delagoa Bay (now known as Maputo, capital of present-day Mozambique). During Dingiswayo's reign there was no Zulu kingdom as such. The 'Zulu' consisted of a number of extended social units, who lived in the south-east of the region between the Mthethwa, under King Dingiswayo, to whom they owed political allegiance, and the powerful King Zwide of the Ndwandwe to the north.

SHAKA

When the growing conflict between the Mthethwa and the Ndwandwe came to a head in 1817, Dingiswayo was captured and killed, but the Ndwandwe did not succeed in destroying the budding Zulu state, which was by then already under the leadership of Shaka kaSenzangakhona. As a tributary of the Mthethwa, Shaka had been encouraged to create a firm regional basis of resistance to the Ndwandwe and, some time in 1819, he managed to defeat Zwide with the assistance of several other chiefdoms. Within a period of some twelve years, Shaka, with his unwavering determination, iron discipline and ruthless leadership, was able to create one of the most formidable fighting forces in Africa. However, recent research suggests that Shaka was also a man of his times: like other leaders in south-east Africa in the early nineteenth century, including the newly defeated Zwide of the Ndwandwe and Matiwane of the Ngwane, he owed his position not only to his aggressive style of leadership and his ability to make quick decisions, but also to his diplomatic and organizational skills.

During Shaka's reign white people began to play an increasingly prominent role in the history of the region. In 1824 they arrived at the bay of Port Natal, which is now known as Durban. Under the leadership of James King and Francis Farewell, a party of hunters, traders and adventurers came to explore the commercial potential of links with the Zulu state. While many historians agree that the whites probably had little impact on Zulu affairs at that time, it appears that Shaka was quite intrigued by them and went to some lengths to impress upon them the power and wealth of his kingdom. He even gave them title to land around Port Natal. It is from the writings of some of these early travellers that much of the subsequent information about the Zulu nation is gleaned. Shaka took the whites on hunting expeditions and some of those early adventurers in fact witnessed his last vicious clash with and defeat of his old northern rival, King Zwide of the Ndwandwe. However, Shaka's main expansionist ambitions were to the south, and he moved his capital from kwaBuluwayo, 'the place of killing', to Dukuza, not far north of Port Natal.

DINGANE

Shaka was finally assassinated by his half-brothers Dingane and Mhalangana in 1828 and, after some bitter quarrelling, Dingane gained ascendance and the leadership of the Zulu empire. Apparently Dingane was a very different person from his half-brother; he had neither Shaka's military brilliance nor his expansionist ambitions. In addition, he lacked the leadership qualities to hold together the still immature state system which Shaka had developed. Rebel chiefs began to break away, and Dingane did not have the skill to force them back.

By this time, the majority of the original whites were no longer there. They had been replaced by a growing group of mostly elephant hunters and adventurers, who proved to be both scheming and quarrelsome. Dingane was, however, more alarmed at the arrival of a completely different group of whites. These were the Voortrekkers, a group of disgruntled white farmers, known as the 'Boers', who were descendants of the Dutch, German and French who had settled at the Cape of Good Hope in the seventeenth and eighteenth centuries. Following the British occupation of the Cape, the Boers emigrated in their ox-wagons, in a movement known as the Great Trek, into the interior. Some of them crossed the Drakensberg mountains to set up temporary camps close to Zulu territory, and one group, led by Piet Retief, negotiated with Dingane for

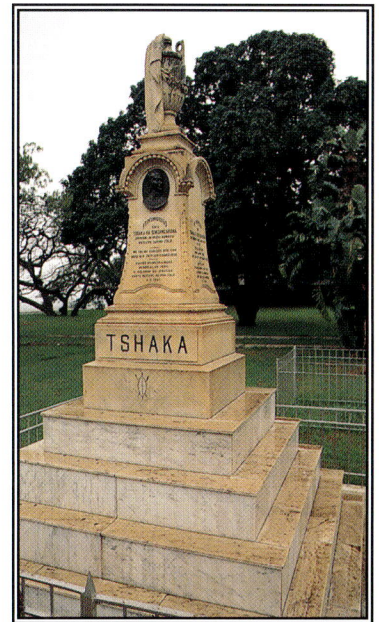

OPPOSITE: Prince Gilenja, a patriarch of the Biyela group. The prince's family have played a significant role in Zulu politics since the days of Shaka, his grandfather having fought against the British at the battle of Isandlwana. Gilenja himself, who was a warrior captain in his youth, belongs to an age regiment named Pondo lwendlovu *(elephant tusk).*
ABOVE: A monument to the mighty King Shaka at Stanger in KwaZulu-Natal.

BELOW: *A few artefacts that were used by the Boers during their confrontations with the Zulu in the nineteenth century.*
RIGHT: *The Blood River monument close to Dundee in KwaZulu-Natal. During this battle, the Ncome River turned red with blood as hundreds of wounded Zulu warriors tried to escape from the Boers.*

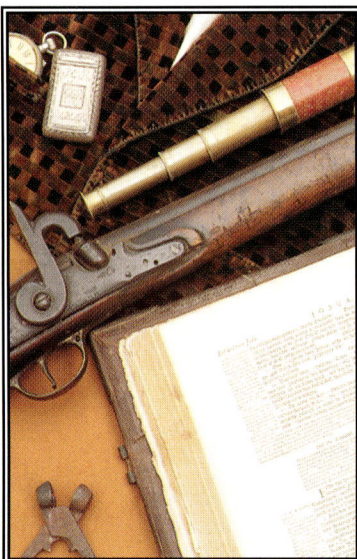

permanent land on which to settle. However, Dingane was fearful that this group of whites, with their huge herds of cattle, military skills and lack of respect for black chiefs, would eventually topple him from his throne. When Retief and seventy of his followers attended Dingane's residence at eMgungundlovu on 6 February 1838 for a celebratory dance, they were clubbed to death and impaled on the orders of the king. What followed was a series of brutal attacks by the Zulu on the Boer encampments, which in turn were followed by revenge attacks by the Boers.

The apprehensive British traders at Port Natal allowed the temptation of a chance to loot Dingane's cattle, as well as their desire to support their fellow white settlers, to lure them into the war on the side of the Boers. Dingane was unable to exterminate the Boers totally, and was finally defeated at the famous Battle of Blood River on the banks of the Ncome River on 16 December 1838.

On that day, so many Zulu were repulsed back into the river that it became choked with corpses and stained with blood. It has been known as Blood River ever since. After this humiliating defeat, Dingane's power was irreparably damaged, but his dispirited

army was defeated finally by his own remaining half-brother, Mpande, who had built a powerful following. Mpande's army, assisted by the Boers, attacked Dingane on the Maqongqo Hills close to the Swaziland border. Dingane fled, but was killed, the exact details of his death being unknown.

MPANDE

As a young man, Mpande had been dismissed as a harmless simpleton, yet he helped to steer the Zulu kingdom through a time of unprecedentedly rapid and far-reaching political change. In contrast to Shaka, Mpande was not a great warrior, but during his rule the Zulu enjoyed a relatively peaceful period of their history. He reigned for 30 years – longer than the other kings put together – and died a natural death in 1872.

Following the Battle of Blood River, two years of conflict ensued for the Zulu kingdom. Many individual chiefs, dissatisfied with the state of affairs, moved out of the

ABOVE: The graves of Coghill and Melville, two British soldiers who fell at Fugitives' Drift in January 1879.

Zulu kingdom to the Colony of Natal. The Boers had taken approximately 30,000 head of cattle for helping Mpande to defeat Dingane and, in addition to that, they claimed the land as far as the Black Mfolozi, which in effect amounted to two thirds of the Zulu kingdom. This explains why, despite Mpande's skills in dealing with increasingly large numbers of traders, settlers and missionaries, many contemporary Zulu accuse him of having betrayed the Zulu nation. In 1842, when the British decided to exercise their claim to the Colony of Natal, most of the Trekkers withdrew to the north where they established the Transvaal Republic in 1852. After that time, the Colony posed an ongoing threat to the Zulu kingdom.

The black population of the Colony of Natal grew from around 100,000 in 1845 to approximately 305,000 in 1872. It is not clear to what extent this growth was fuelled by refugees from the Zulu kingdom. In the early 1840s, many people who had never been fully assimilated into Zulu society chose to leave the kingdom, but it is unlikely that the problem of returning refugees had any signifcant impact on King Mpande's reign in later years. Prevented from expanding to the south by the presence of increasingly large settler communities, Mpande's military expeditions were restricted to raids on tributary chiefdoms to the north-west of his kingdom. He also tried, unsuccessfully, to bring large tracts of southern Swaziland under Zulu control in 1846. The Swazi, who initially sought refuge in caves, soon entered into an alliance with a party of Voortrekkers, who forced Mpande to withdraw. When Mpande died in late 1872, he was buried at his royal homestead, Nodwengu, in the Valley of the Kings on the Mahlabatini Plains, and was succeeded by his son, Cetshwayo.

CETSHWAYO

Under Cetshwayo many changes were made to the Zulu army. The warriors were not permanently mobilized and, even once the units had been established, they were allowed to spend long periods of time at home with their families, and would be called up only when the need arose. By that stage, in the aftermath of the Napoleonic wars, firearms were available to the Zulu army in large quantities. Guns had first fallen into the hands of the Zulu during the wars with the Voortrekkers in the 1830s, and Mpande had tried to obtain more, in an attempt to strengthen his position against Dingane. Cetshwayo now needed guns in order to secure his position within his kingdom, and many thousands of guns are said to have come into the area through the Portuguese traders at Delagoa Bay.

Cetshwayo succeeded in persuading the Colony of Natal to recognize him as the legitimate Zulu king, but for this he later had to pay a price. In his capacity as ruler of the Zulu, he also refused to negotiate with the Boers in the Transvaal Republic over a border dispute. While he had managed to strengthen the Zulu army once more, many of the more powerful chiefs began to resist a return to the centralized state power which had existed during the reigns of Shaka and Dingane. This meant that the strength of the Zulu state was considerably weaker than during Shaka's time, a position which exacerbated issues during the war of 1879.

As Cetshwayo revitalized the Zulu army, so this sent waves of apprehension through colonial Natal. At the same time, the growing power of the Zulu came to be seen as a major threat to the British Imperial forces, with their vision of an Empire of English control across Africa, extending from the Cape in the south to Cairo in the far north. War became inevitable. As Ian Knight has pointed out, the invasion of the Zulu kingdom in 1879 was 'portrayed . . . as a preventative campaign waged against a cruel

and bloodthirsty despot and his army'. Most historians, however, now accept this view as the propaganda it was, and suggest that the causes of the war lay rather in a British desire to simplify the complex political situation in southern Africa by joining the disparate British and Boer states together in a federation. A large independent Zulu state was seen as a threat to this scheme.

The result was that the British conspired against the Zulu, by seizing upon minor border incidents, following which they presented King Cetshwayo with a stiff ultimatum. This included a demand that he disband the Zulu military system. The Zulu, although well aware of the gravity of the situation, ignored the ultimatum, at which point the British crossed the border, invading the Zulu kingdom on 11 January 1879.

BELOW: A view over Fugitives' Drift, where the Zulu and British went to battle in 1879.

On or about 17 January of that same year, the assembled Zulu army of more than 20,000 warriors, after having been doctored for war according to tradition, marched from Ondini, Cetshwayo's capital, to confront Lord Chelmsford's army, and defend their territory. The Zulu attacked the British camp at Isandlwana, advancing from the surrounding hills, and caught the British scattered over a wide plain in front of the camp. The British opened fire but were finally overcome. The Zulu then moved on to attack the supply depot at Rorke's Drift. The British had been warned by the survivors of Isandlwana that the Zulu were approaching, and barricaded the two mission stations with biscuit boxes and maize bags. But, despite the fact that approximately 4,000 warriors, led by Prince Dabulamanzi, continued to assault the post from five in the afternoon until after midnight, they could not dislodge the British. Finally, on 23 January, the attack was called off.

BELOW: The peaceful scene of the Rorke's Drift mission and old cattle enclosure, where, more than a hundred years ago, Zulu warriors and British soldiers clashed in a bloody battle.

Lord Chelmsford lost 850 of his white troops and 400 black men from the Colony of Natal, who had been recruited to fight their old enemies in the Zulu kingdom. The Zulu, although they had exacted a great victory over the British, had lost more than 1,000 warriors at Isandlwana and 400 at Rorke's Drift. Ian Knight describes the aftermath of the battles: 'The (Zulu) survivors tried to bury the bodies in dongas (gullies), ant-bear holes, or in the grain pits of nearby homesteads, but the numbers were so great that many had to be left on the field with just a shield to cover them. They then dispersed to their homes, taking their wounded with them – hundreds of men suffering injuries from heavy calibre bullets, which were beyond the skills of the *izinyanga* or traditional healers'. Many more Zulu lives were lost at the ensuing battles of Khambula and eMgungundlovu, shattering Cetshwayo's strategic plans and the morale of the Zulu army, who were up against the world's most efficient army at the time, the British Imperial Forces. Cetshwayo stepped up his attempts to reach a diplomatic solution with the invading British forces. However, by this stage the British were interested in talking peace only once they had avenged their humiliating defeat at the hands of the Zulu at Isandlwana. Even though they knew their situation was hopeless, the Zulu continued to resist the British in a number of skirmishes, during which the young Prince Imperial of France, the exiled heir to the Bonapartist throne who was in the region as an observer, was killed by a Zulu scouting party.

THE BATTLE OF ULUNDI

Lord Chelmsford, on the warpath to crush the Zulu, finally drew up his army on the Mahlabatini Plains in the vicinity of Cetshwayo's capital, Ondini. On the morning of 4 July 1879, he crossed the White Mfolozi River, razing Ondini to the ground. More than 6,000 Zulu died and thousands of cattle were driven off by the British. The

political, military, social and economic structure of the great Zulu empire was shattered. King Cetshwayo was taken captive, and the Zulu nation was divided by the British into thirteen small chiefdoms, in an attempt to dismantle the Zulu state, and to exploit existing divisions within the kingdom. Cetshwayo was imprisoned in the former Cape Province, from where he petitioned to be allowed to return to his kingdom. In September 1881, the dignified King Cetshwayo was allowed to visit London to state his case. Having dined with Queen Victoria and made a favourable impression upon the Imperial administrators, he was finally given permission to return home. He landed on the coast of Zululand in 1883.

In the meanwhile, the imposed divisions in Zululand had led to a smouldering civil war and a period of continuing strife. This resulted in increasing intervention of the then Natal Colonial administration in the government and control of Zulu affairs. Cetshwayo, stripped of all his power, watched in helpless misery as violence erupted across the country. Not only was he not in a position to assist, but the British blamed him for provoking it.

Things finally came to a head when an old Zulu rival, Zibhebhu, and his Mandhlakazi *impi* (regiments) bore down on Cetshwayo's rebuilt royal homestead on the morning of 21 July, sacking it and killing fifty-nine of his *izinduna* (headmen).

The wounded King Cetshwayo managed to escape to the remote hills above the Tugela River. He later tried to salvage something of the Zulu fortunes but, while he was in the process of petitioning the British magistracy at Eshowe, he suddenly became ill, and died. The official cause of his death was given as heart disease, but there have always been suspicions that he was in fact poisoned.

DINUZULU

Not yet a teenager, Cetshwayo's son, Dinuzulu, became king. Acting as regents until he came of age, Prince Ndabuko kaMpande – Cetshwayo's full brother – and Chief Mnyamana, of the Buthelezi lineage, petitioned the British for help against the Mandhlakazi. When this failed to materialize, they turned to the Boers of the former Transvaal Republic, who promised help against the marauding enemy. The Boers proclaimed Dinuzulu king – which the British refused to acknowledge – before heading off to attack Zibhebhu's warriors. In return for their services to King Dinuzulu, the Boers claimed farms, stretching across the length of Zululand.

Once again the Zulu appealed to the British for assistance. This time they did respond, possibly motivated more out of fear that the Boers would establish a route from the Transvaal Republic to the sea, than out of a willingness to assist the Zulu king in his straitened circumstances.

Zululand was finally annexed by the British on 9 May 1887, bringing the area under the control of the Colony of Natal's Native Law, and magistrates were established throughout Zululand. Dinuzulu attempted to restore his authority, but ultimately he was thwarted by the magistrates, by land disputes and by further attacks from Zibhebhu's Mandhlakazi. In spite of some initial success by his *uSuthu* (followers) against Zibhebhu and the whites, the British defeated him and his warriors at Hlopekulu Mountain near Ulundi. King Dinuzulu and some of his leaders were caught, tried for treason and exiled to St Helena Island.

This rebellion of 1888 marked the real end of the old Zulu military system and the power of the Zulu kings. With the exception of one last tragic uprising by rebel forces, this was also the last time the Zulu Royal House went to war.

King Solomon, who was Dinuzulu's son and successor, lived through a period of dynamic transition in the political role of the Zulu kingship. King Solomon founded the first Inkatha movement in the mid-1920s in an attempt to rally support for the institution of Zulu kingship, not only among Zulu-speakers from the area formerly under the control of Shaka and his successors, but also among the increasingly educated Christian African community (*amakholwa*) in the former Natal. In the years leading up to King Solomon's death in 1933, this Inkatha movement was undermined by corruption and a lack of political direction. King Solomon's son and successor, Cyprian, who was forced to fulfil the role of a consitutional monarch, rather than a political leader, nevertheless succeeded in forging a strong alliance with his cousin and adviser, Chief Buthelezi, who had an enormous influence on the course of Zulu politics following his return from the University of Fort Hare in 1953.

When Cyprian died in 1968, Chief Buthelezi became an increasingly important political figure, thwarting the apartheid government's attempts to impose Bantustan policies on Zululand, and mobilizing the support of the majority of Zulu-speakers through the formation of a second Inkatha movement, founded in 1975. Assisted by the present Zulu king, Goodwill Zwelithini, Buthelezi revived a number of rituals that were last practised during the reigns of King Shaka and his immediate successors. He also introduced several new ones, such as the annual Reed Ceremony, derived from a Swazi ritual, and encouraged his followers to adopt forms of dress associated with the proud military heritage of the Zulu kingdom. As a result of this, large numbers of Zulu-speakers have renewed their interest in Zulu history during the late twentieth century.

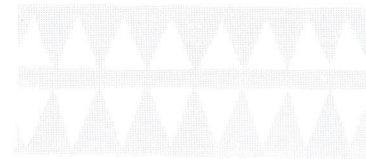

BELOW: Some traditional Zulu weapons: spears and battle axes.

HOMESTEADS

Ezomndeni
Family matters

Before the introduction of the cash economy into Zulu society in the early twentieth century, Zulu people relied on nature for food and shelter. Harvesting of natural resources is still practised in rural areas by people whose expertise was handed down to them by their forefathers. While much remains as it has been for centuries, things are changing as people adapt to new influences and developments.

RIGHT: Building methods have changed over the years, but many Zulu homes are still built out of locally available natural materials. Walls may be smeared with a mixture of mud and manure, and roofs are thatched.
OPPOSITE: Traditionally women thatch their houses, but these days, while the men are working in the cities, women also undertake strenuous work such as actually building the houses.

A traditional homestead (*umuzi*) is a cluster of dwellings, home to a married man (*umnumzane*) and his family. The *umnumzane* is undisputed head of the household, and may in the past have had two or more wives depending on how wealthy he was. Until children married, they lived with their parents, and relatives (widowed parents or unmarried sisters and their children) sometimes also lived in the *umuzi*. A Zulu family was close-knit, with tasks divided along gender lines and in order of seniority. These days, even in the rural areas of KwaZulu-Natal, polygyny is not as common as it used to be, but it is still common among some chiefs, who rely on the people in their wards to provide the cattle for their bride wealth (*see* Men, page 76).

A large cluster of individual households, comprising up to 800 *imizi*, falls under a lower-order chief (*induna*). Clusters within a geographical region usually fall under the administration of a more important chief (*inkosi*) who, in the past, owed allegiance directly to the Zulu monarch.

Historically land was not owned by individuals but administered by the *inkosi*. Today large areas of grazing are still communal; they are not owned by any one person and must be applied for through the local chief. Residential land was allocated to married men and use of it was inherited by the male progeny. In the past land was very seldom passed down to a woman, but under South Africa's new constitution, in terms of which people may not be discriminated against on the basis of gender, it has become increasingly common for land (usually residential, with little if any agricultural land) to be allocated to single mothers. In some areas, when a man was allocated land near an existing *umuzi*, the established inhabitant would stand at the gate of his *umuzi* and throw four stones in the directions of the compass points. Where the stones landed showed the newcomer where he should start building.

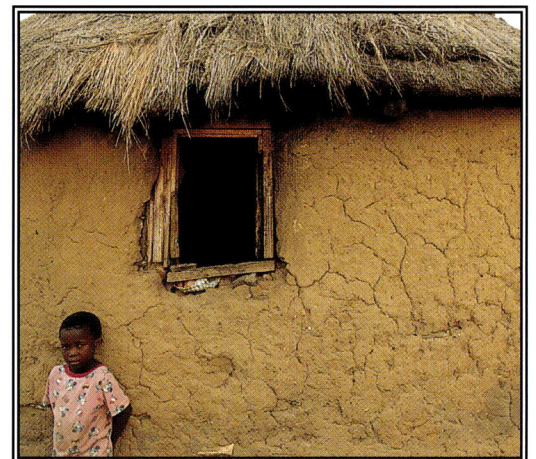

A traditional Zulu *umuzi* is circular in shape, consisting of a number of round homes encircled by a stockade made of tamboti wood, which is poisonous to insects. The stockade was high, to prevent wild animals such as lion from jumping over the barrier and attacking people and livestock. These days, since there are few wild animals roving free, people do not bother to build stockades. A hedge or a small fence usually suffices to demarcate the homestead and prevents goats and cattle from straying.

Ideally, an *umuzi* was built facing down a slope, with its entrance at the lowest point. This provided a good vantage point and protection from possible attacks by enemies, as well as helping with drainage. Agricultural crops were usually planted outside the fence on the slope below the *umuzi*. During heavy rains, manure and nutrients from the cattle enclosure inside the *umuzi* would flow down into the fields, fertilizing the crops.

For hundreds of years the Zulu lived in beehive houses: circular, domed structures made from sapling and grass. These dwellings *(izindlu)* were well suited to the environment: well insulated and warm in the bitterly cold winters of inland KwaZulu-Natal, and cool in the blistering hot summers. They were about three metres (10 feet) in diameter, but those belonging to people of high status were frequently larger. Homes of high-ranking people could easily be distinguished: only the best reeds and materials would have been used, and the weaving and workmanship would have been more intricate.

The actual building was traditionally the man's responsibility, and men from nearby *imizi* would come together to help their neighbours build a new home. The harvesting of thatching grass to cover the structure fell to the women's lot. The grass was harvested when the stems were long and still fairly pliable. The women would weave the ropes and mats used for building, and would also weave the top notch of the house. The mats were gradually wound around the sapling framework, from the bottom to the top. A second layer was later added, and finally the house was thatched by the women. To waterproof and neaten the appearance, all the thatching mats and grass were bound and secured with a web of grass rope. Floors were plastered with a mixture of cow dung and ant-heap soil, which was smeared on the ground and polished with large pebbles to a smooth and shiny gloss. There were no windows in the home and only one low door. Oral tradition suggests that doorways were low in order to repel intruders – any person entering the house would have to stoop which placed him at a disadvantage.

While there are many advantages to a home constructed in this traditional manner, the early Zulu had to contend with a number of problems. In highland areas notorious for electric storms, fire was a serious threat. This hazard was increased by the presence of a central, indoor fire used for cooking and keeping warm during inclement weather. Insects could also pose a problem, as they could wreak havoc in a home made from

BELOW AND BOTTOM LEFT: The old-style beehive houses have largely been replaced by homes built in the wattle and daub tradition. Each family brings an individual touch to their home, be it in the colour of paint, decorative motifs or thatching details. Many traditionalists still build one beehive structure (the grandmother's house) in their umuzi, *in the belief that the ancestors might otherwise not be able to recognize their earthly homes.*

BOTTOM RIGHT: Although houses are not always built in traditional styles, many rural people still dress in their traditional regalia on special occasions.

ABOVE: Houses are often built using locally available wood, stone and thatching grass. The houses are plastered over with a mixture of soil, cattle manure and cement, and then decorated with colourful paints.

natural materials, by eating away at the saplings and dried grass. Furthermore creatures such as spiders, rodents and even snakes would make their homes in the warm and cosy Zulu homes. The construction and maintenance of these structures was extremely labour-intensive and time-consuming. The expected life span of a traditional dwelling is estimated at between two and eight years, before it needs major re-thatching, or even total reconstruction. This, however, would obviously depend on the quality of the materials used, the skills of the builder, and the climatic conditions of the area.

While an indoor fire may pose a fire hazard, the smoke from the fire blackened the internal structural saplings, protecting the wood against sparks which could otherwise easily ignite the home. The soot also provided protection against insects and other destructive vermin. Seed mielies (maize), set aside for the following year's planting, were often stored in the smoky rafters of the hut where they were protected from termites.

The introduction of modern building materials and methods of construction has modified some traditional gender-specific tasks around a Zulu household. For instance, more of the building of houses, as well as maintenance of the home, is left in the hands of rural women now than in the past, although men still undertake the heavier part of the construction if they are home from their jobs in the cities or on the mines. In rural areas, many of the simpler *imizi* still consist of circular dwellings made from wood and thatch but, more often than not, houses these days have walls made from wattle poles and stones plastered over with cattle manure and clay. Alternatively, depending on how wealthy the home owner is, blocks and bricks may be used. While the layout of the

BELOW: Nyama Ndlovu and Ncanana weaving a gate. Doors and fences are also woven using young saplings.
BOTTOM: Even chicken coops in rural areas are built in the traditional beehive style.
RIGHT: Women sort the long thatching grass and weave mats that will be used to build a traditional beehive house.

umuzi remains essentially unaltered, the houses are more likely to be rectangular than circular in shape, although this too would depend on income: a round house can be built cheaply with locally available material, but the blocks and cement that are needed for a rectangular, modern house make it more expensive. Where thatching grass is readily available and cheap, it is still used for roofing, but today many prefer corrugated galvanized roofing. It may lack the aesthetic appeal and insulation qualities of thatch, but it is far less labour-intensive to erect and maintain, and less of a fire hazard.

THE CATTLE BYRE

In the centre of every *umuzi* is the all-important cattle byre *(isibaya)*. Cattle represent a Zulu family's bank balance, and as a result the cattle are always kept secure. However, the cattle byre is more than just a place where the cattle are kept at night. It is the sacred place where the head of the household is buried, and consequently it is also believed to be one of the places where the male ancestors of a family reside. To keep the ancestors informed of earthly events, important announcements are made in the *isibaya*. Sacrifices are also offered here.

The ancestors can be described as the spirits of the deceased members of a family who can intervene in the spirit world on behalf of the living members of the family. This power means that the ancestors are held in considerable awe and are accorded great importance. They need to be acknowledged, appeased and informed of any special occasions or planned changes in the lives of the family or larger community. Sacrifices of goats and sometimes cattle facilitate communication with the ancestors. More often than not, this takes place inside the cattle byre. Just as in life there are good and bad people, so there are good and bad ancestors. Sacrifices are usually made only to those ancestors who people consider were good and kind when they were alive, or to those ancestors to whom a person was close during their lifetime (*see also page 140*).

Only the head of the household is buried inside the cattle byre. Family members are usually buried outside the perimeter of the *umuzi* at a special site. The *umnumzane* always used to be buried in a sitting position, since it was felt that, if buried lying down, he might fall asleep and forget to look after the family. Today people are usually buried in coffins, and the practice of burying people sitting up has largely fallen away. Whether buried sitting or lying in a coffin, it is imperative that the *umnumzane* be buried facing the most important dwelling in the *umuzi*, the grandmother's house. It is also important that his head should be in the shade of a buffalo thorn tree *(umlahlankosi)*, which the Zulu believe attracts good ancestral spirits. Many different animals love to eat from the *umlahlankosi*, which may explain why the Zulu regard it highly.

BELOW: Traditionally the cattle byre, which is built in the centre of the umuzi, *is surrounded by a tall wooden stockade of tamboti wood, which protects the animals from theft or marauding wild animals which might otherwise come into the* umuzi.

BELOW AND BOTTOM LEFT: The care of children is often shared in a modern polygynous household.
BOTTOM RIGHT: Victor '2 Bullet' Zakwe from the Mchunu district in Msinga, a very traditional area, being served by his wife. In rural KwaZulu-Natal, a married woman, who may be identified by her headgear, still serves men in the hlonipha *fashion – kneeling, her eyes lowered and not raising her head higher than that of the* umnumzane. *'2 Bullet' is part of Victor's praise name, derived from the days of faction fighting for which the Msinga/Tugela area is remembered.*

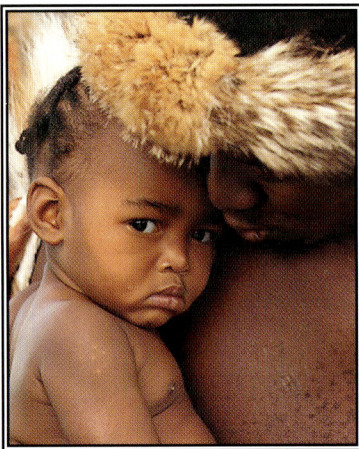

With the introduction of Christianity (*see* page 155), polygyny is less prevalent these days in Zulu society than it used to be, although it is still practised in some places. In the past, polygyny provided a balance in a society where the death rate among males was far higher than among females. From when they were very young, boys were sent out to herd and guard the family's cattle. The environment was harsh and, by the time young men went into military training, the gender ratios were already severely out of kilter. Many men were killed in the various Zulu wars and, when those who survived were finally released from military service and were granted permission to marry, polygyny provided a fairly natural social solution to the gender imbalance of the time.

Everyone in a Zulu household is assigned a specific role in the social system, which theoretically should reduce squabbling and in-fighting between family members, but, as is the way with human beings, this is not always the case. In spite of this, many Zulu people today continue to support and ascribe to the patrilineal system of succession that has been in place in Zulu culture for centuries.

In traditional polygynous society, the great or chief wife (*inkosikazi*) is not necessarily a man's first wife; in the case of important chiefs, the *inkosikazi* is chosen in consultation with the elders. Her first-born son is chief successor and heir to his father and he is always the most important son in the *umuzi*. Similarly, her first-born daughter is the most important daughter. Should the great wife fail to produce a male heir, the first-born son of the second chief wife (*inqadi*) would be heir to the *umnumzane*.

From the day he is born, the first son of the first or great wife in modern households is groomed for his role as heir to his father's estate. Even if he is weak in any way, his role in the community or his succession rights are unlikely to be openly challenged. With their belief in external spiritual control over their lives (*see* The Metaphysical World, page 140), Zulu people tend to accept that destiny has placed an individual in a certain position for a specific reason.

The first son of the first wife inherits the family's cattle but, if the first wife does not bear a son, the first son (never a girl) of the second wife fills this position. If a man fails to produce a son with any of his wives, his brothers or brothers' sons inherit the cattle and assume responsibility for the family. When a man dies, his wife resides with her last-born son, who will inherit whatever cattle were given to her at the time of her marriage. When there is a third wife, her son often acts as appeal court in family disputes.

THE TRADITIONAL *UMUZI*

The social structure of a traditional Zulu extended homestead *(umuzi)* may be considered a microcosm of the wider society: in the *umuzi* the roles of all the individuals and their relationships to each other correspond to the greater Zulu society.

The most important house in an *umuzi* was that of the grandmother, or of the great wife. This was usually the largest house, built opposite to (facing) the entrance of the *umuzi*. This is often also known as the ancestors' house *(indlu yangenhla)* as it is believed that the ancestors reside here. In the past, this house was also used as the schoolroom: at their grandmother's feet children would learn about the history of their family, the area in which they lived and other important issues. Rituals in honour of the ancestors were held in this house on special occasions, such as weddings, coming of age ceremonies or when someone died. A goat or cow would usually be slaughtered outside in the cattle byre and the entrails cooked and eaten in the ancestors' house, to appease the spirits of the ancestors. Spoons, meat plates and other utensils that are used to eat the food obtained from these cattle (and are thus associated with the ancestors) are stored in the rafters of the grandmother's home.

TOP: The Zulu umuzi, *built on a slope in a circular fashion, is home to an extended family. The cattle byre is always central, with crops grown on the periphery.*
ABOVE: The formal education of Zulu children has resulted in many changes in traditional Zulu society.
FOLLOWING PAGES: Imizi *nestle close to the river in the beautiful rural area near Eshowe.*

TOP LEFT, MIDDLE AND ABOVE:
When a baby is born, a goat is
often sacrificed to the ancestors. A
small piece of goatskin is wound
into a bracelet and placed on the
baby's wrist, as a sign that this
ceremony has been performed.
TOP RIGHT: Zulu women and
children gather around the
central fire in a modern home.
OPPOSITE TOP: In traditional
society Zulu children are taught
from a very early age to respect
their elders. Here a small girl
walks with her mother who wears
the traditional head-dress of a
married woman.
OPPOSITE BOTTOM: The inside
of a young girl's house (ilawu)
is decorated with the help of her
mother. She will entertain her
friends and, eventually, her
boyfriend in her ilawu.

The second chief wife *(inqadi)*, who had a supplementary role to the *inkosikazi*, was accorded much importance. Her house was in the place of honour on the right-hand side of the *umuzi*. To the left, was the home of the *ikhohlo* or left-hand wife. Should the *umnumzane* have more wives, the third wife's house would be on the right-hand side and so on, odd numbers on the left and even numbers on the right. All those on the left would fall under the *inqadi*, and those on the right under the *ikhohlo*, although all of them would ultimately be under the *umnumzane* and the *inkosikazi*.

Apart from the house of the grandmother (or great wife) and the private house of the *umnumzane*, if he had one, the houses were all constructed similarly, with sparse furnishings. Each section of the *umuzi* usually had its own small beehive enclosures for storing grain, vegetables or beer, which were between the houses and the outer fence. Inside, the houses were divided into male and female sections. At the top end of the *umuzi*, usually near the grandmother's house, furthest from the entrance, was the *umsamo*, a sacred area which, like the cattle enclosure, was considered a special area where the ancestral spirits dwelt. Eating utensils, pots of beer and maize, and valuables were stored in the *umsamo*, into which only the *umnumzane* and his wife might go. In the centre of each house was the fireplace.

At night, sleeping mats were unrolled and placed on the floor. During the day they were rolled up and kept in decorative holders *(umgibe)* on the walls. Women always slept on the left-hand side of the homestead, and men on the right. One explanation given for this is that a man holds his shield on his left arm, leaving his right hand free to grab his spear; so, if a man were attacked in his home, he could quickly grab his weapons with his right hand.

The *umnumzane* slept in the house of whichever of his wives he wished to. However, if he wanted to keep the peace, he would divide his attention equally among them. Often, men of status would have a house of their own, where he could entertain his friends, hold meetings in inclement weather, or generally keep out of the way of the women and children when he so desired.

The children slept in their mother's house until they were old enough to move to a single-sex 'dormitory' near the gate of the *umuzi*. Children would be moved here once parents realized that their off-spring's 'eyes were opening' – the children were aware of what happened on the nights when their father came to stay with their mother. It was quite a tricky business for parents to get together while children were sleeping nearby. Usually they would wait for the children to fall asleep, and then the *umnumzane* would throw a small stone at his wife, or prod her with a long stick kept conveniently on his side of the house, indicating to her that she should join him. In modern times, conventional beds have largely replaced the old sleeping mats but, in some rural areas, the male and female sides of the house and the *umsamo* are still respected and maintained.

The older children's dormitories are also still a feature in many rural *imizi* today. Historically they would have been situated away from the other inhabitants, the girls' dormitory on the left-hand side of the *umuzi* and that of the boys on the right near the gate. The boys are positioned on the right for a similar reason to that given to explain why men sleep on the right-hand side of the homestead: from their position near the entrance, the older sons would be better able to protect the *umuzi*. As a young man approached marriageable age, he would often be given his own homestead away from the dormitory, where he could entertain his friends and have some measure of privacy.

FEEDING THE FAMILY

The ancestors of the present-day Zulu people were pastoralists, who kept large herds of cattle. In this patrilineal society, where cattle continue to play a significant role, the important task of tending and managing the herds has always traditionally fallen to the

men and boys' lot. The young boys would take the cattle out to the fields at dawn, and bring them back at mid-morning to be milked. Zulu people traditionally seldom drank fresh milk, preferring curdled milk *(amasi)* which was prepared in gourds and eaten daily, either on its own or with stiff lumpy maize porridge *(uphuthu)*.

Agricultural tasks (tilling the fields and producing crops), considered less important or menial, were performed by the women. Each woman was allocated a small plot of ground where she would cultivate crops such as Zulu pumpkin, *amadumbe* (a potato-like tuber), sweet potatoes, ground-nuts, beans and melons. Many other food crops, such as Zulu spinach *(imfino)*, were harvested wild in the surrounding areas. Maize is one of the major staple foods, and sorghum and millet, which are used to make beer, are grown in some areas. The system of migrant labour has to some extent led to a break-down of traditional divisions of labour, and these days, while the men are away on the mines or urban centres, many rural women have to look after the household's cattle.

Grain used to be stored in small enclosures on stilts, where children and animals could not get to it, and where it was ventilated in humid weather. In times of upheaval, it would be stored in underground pits in the centre of the cattle byre, to prevent enemies from stealing or burning it. This practice is still used in some rural areas today.

Meat was considered a luxury in traditional Zulu society, and was seldom eaten by the ordinary people. Their cattle were too valuable to be slaughtered as a matter of course, but were kept for feast days, or for ceremonies and important sacrifices. Zulu monarchs organized and undertook spectacular hunts of wild game, particularly of designated royal species such as elephant. However, hunting on that scale was time-consuming and

dangerous, and was principally undertaken on special occasions or when necessity demanded it. Traditionally, hunting took place in the drier winter months when the grass was shorter and game easier to spot. At this time of the year animals also tend to congregate near water, making them easier to locate. Many rural Zulu men today, who still consider hunting with a rifle most unsporting, spend hours honing their hunting skills with traditional hunting weapons, such as spears, clubs and sticks. They also use dogs in tracking and bringing down an animal.

BOTTOM LEFT: Zulu children carry water in large plastic containers through the fallow agricultural fields, which during the autumn months are covered in purple and pink cosmos flowers.

BELOW, MIDDLE AND BOTTOM RIGHT: Scenes of domesticity around a typical rural Zulu homestead. The sica *(indigenous African domestic dogs) sun themselves, an* inkezo *(calabash) grows among the* amaswela *plants, and a tractor stands in the fields until the ploughing season.*

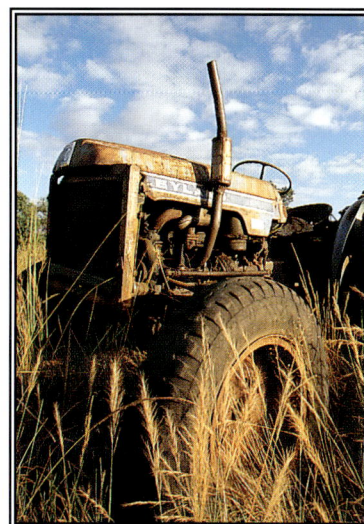

BELOW: Three-legged cast-iron pots, introduced in the mid-nineteenth century, have largely replaced handmade traditional earthen clay pots for cooking.
MIDDLE: The family meal is cooked over an open fire.
BOTTOM LEFT: Pumpkins, a favourite Zulu food, are stored on the corrugated iron roof of a rural home to prevent them from rotting and to keep them away from pigs and other scavengers.
BOTTOM RIGHT: Having harvested plants from their cultivated gardens and from the wild, Zulu women sit inside to prepare the vegetables for the family meal.

In some regions, when the head of a household dies, a hunt forms part of the funeral ceremony, and the widow is given the meat from the hunt. A cow or goat is also slaughtered. In the far northern parts of KwaZulu-Natal, coming home from a hunt with an entire animal is thought to bring bad luck to the hunter's family. To avert ill fortune, the first man to encounter the hunter carrying his kill home will tap him on either shoulder with a spear, and the hunter will hand over a hind quarter of the animal.

MEALTIMES

Good manners, which are fundamental to Zulu society, are most evident at a meal. The women serve the men and guests from a kneeling position, ensuring that their heads are never higher than those of more senior or more important people *(hlonipha)*. The men and guests who are being served receive the food with both hands, which is considered good manners. During the two meals of the day, people traditionally sat on grass mats either indoors or outdoors, depending on the weather. Men and women ate separately, and guests were treated with the utmost regard and hospitality. Today, as in the past, food is prepared and served by the women and girls of a household. It used to be served on tightly woven mats *(isithebe)* or from clay pots. Meat was, and often still is, served on special wooden platters which were made by highly skilled male carvers. People generally ate with their hands, but spoons were sometimes used. Individuals often had their own carved and decorated wooden spoons which, when not in use, were kept in beautifully woven spoon bags, *(impontshi* or *isampompo)*, which were hung inside the house. Adults frequently ate from wooden plates, while little children of both sexes ate away from the adults from a large communal pot, sharing one big spoon.

These days, enamel and aluminium plates and pots have largely replaced wooden platters and grass serving mats, and cast-iron pots tend to be used for cooking rather than the clay pots that were commonly used in the past.

˙TRADITIONAL BEER

Traditional sorghum beer is an integral part of everyday Zulu life. In modern urban situations, it is drunk only during ceremonies or on special occasions, but in rural areas beer is drunk throughout the day, as it has been for hundreds of years. Zulu women are the principal beer makers, some enjoying formidable reputations within their communities for their skills. This beer, made from water, malt and sorghum and maize, with its high nutrient content, is a staple in most Zulu households. It is always available and may be made daily, depending on the size of the household. It has a low alcoholic content (approximately two to three percent) if drunk in the traditional manner – when it is still fresh. The longer it stands, the more alcoholic it becomes.

To make the beer, maize and sorghum is soaked in water until the grains begin to germinate. The grains are then placed between grass mats. Once the grains are dry, they are ground by hand on a flat stone to produce a fairly rough powder. This is cooked like porridge in a pot of water over a fire, after which it is left in big beer pots to cool for a day or two. Malt is poured on top of the mixture, which is then covered to keep it warm while it ferments. In cold weather, this could take up to five days but, in normal warm weather, the beer could be ready to drink within three days.

Today, as in the past, before the beer-drinking commences, the ancestors first have to be thanked and acknowledged. This is done by skimming the foam off the top of the beer with an *isikhetho*, a special straining spoon made from wood or grass, and dripping it into the earth. Even in urban environments, Zulu men still thank the ancestors by spilling foam from commercially made beer onto the ground of the shebeen. Traditional Zulu beer is served in big clay pots which are covered by an *imbenge*, a woven grass lid. Although the sizes of the pots may vary, beer is generally served from two types of pots – the normal sized *ukhamba*, and the small *umancishana*, the 'stingy pot'.

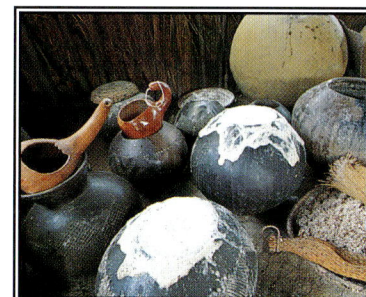

TOP LEFT: After traditional Zulu beer has been brewed, the drinkable part is separated from the husks with a grass strainer.
TOP RIGHT: Once the dry sorghum grains have been ground, they are sifted.
MIDDLE PICTURES: The beer is scooped with a calabash and poured into the strainer.
ABOVE: The beer is left in clay pots to begin the process of fermentation.

ABOVE: Zulu men gather in their ceremonial dress to discuss the events of the day around the pot of beer. Vayisi Biyela, wearing the royal leopard skin, in his younger days saw active service in many faction fights. He is renowned for the powerful war medicines which he uses to confound his enemies. Next to him sits Bhubesi 'the Lion' Shezi who is descended from the lineage who were traditionally spear-makers for Shaka's armies.

Should visitors arrive at an *umuzi* and be served beer from an *umancishana*, they will know that they are not very welcome, or that their host does not wish to share his beer!

On social or ceremonial occasions, Zulu men sit around in a circle and pass the beer pot from one to another, drinking before passing it along. The grass lid covering a beer pot may be lifted only by the headman and, until this has been done, it is extremely impolite to start drinking. Once the beer is finished, the *imbenge* is turned upside down on top of the pot, to signify that the bar is closed. The head of a household usually has his own pot out of which he drinks when he is at home relaxing on his own.

Beer is sometimes used as a means of bartering. During a drought, when an area has crop failures, the raw materials for making beer will be traded between *imizi*. Sometimes beer is used as direct 'payment' for services rendered. For instance, when a new homestead is being built, it is customary for men from the surrounding *imizi* to pitch in. Should the women of the *umuzi* be renowned for their beer-making skills, the chances are good that many more strong hands than usual will be available to help!

ZULU POTS

Mashwabede and Give walk behind the laden donkey. The two women have spent the morning with the children down at the river digging clay from the river bank. Back at home, Mashwabede off-loads the sacks of clay and lays it out on reed mats to dry. Taking a little of the raw clay, she wets it, rolls it into balls and presses it into the eager hands of the waiting boys. Delighted, they start forming the clay into little cows which they leave to bake in the sun before adding them to their collection of other clay cattle. The girls watch carefully as Give takes some of the clay clods which have already dried, and starts grinding them on her heavy grindstone.

Many rural Zulu women are adept at pot-making, and among them a few are known in their community as master potters. Mashwabede and Give are both well known for their pot-making skills, but they also spend much time teaching the children of the *umuzi* how to use the clay. Making pots is exclusively a female occupation, just as wood carving is exclusively done by males. Most potters learn as girls by watching their mothers and grandmothers making pots. The only time that males will make objects out of clay is when they are small boys.

While every Zulu household uses clay pots for a variety of purposes, not every woman knows how to make them. Not all women know where good clay can be obtained, nor which is the best clay needed for a specific type of pot. Fortunately there are still women such as Mashwabede who are happy to share their skills with others. Women from various areas may use different types of clay or methods of firing to produce a diversity of effects, but all Zulu pots are shaped by coiling the clay.

Once the clay has been collected from the river banks and dried, it is ground to a fine powder to which water is added to make a thick paste. To make the base of a pot, the potter flattens on the palm of her hand a small ball of the wet clay which she sets aside. The rest of the clay she rolls into fat sausages or 'snakes' and, from the base, she starts coiling the clay into the shape required. Once she has finished, and while the clay

BOTTOM LEFT: Bags of clay, which is collected from the banks of the river, are transported to the homestead on the backs of donkeys.
BELOW: The clay is rolled into 'snakes' and pressed into the shape of a pot.
BOTTOM RIGHT: While the clay pot is still wet, it is decorated by hand.

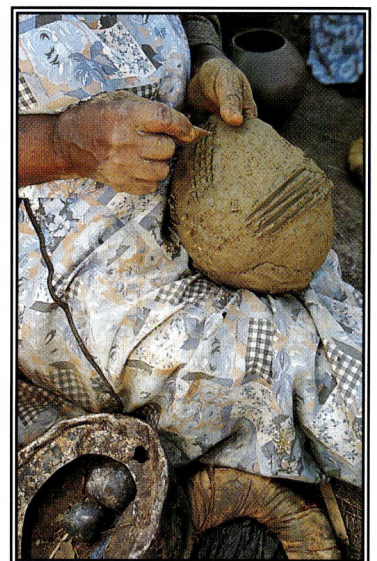

is still wet, she makes a criss-cross or other design on the side of the pot. Beer pots are most commonly patterned on the side, to give the pot a grip which will prevent it from slipping out of the user's hands. They are also decorated for aesthetic reasons, since they are handed around to guests, who must be given the best of everything.

Clay from different areas has different colours when dried – it may be a yellowish mustard or greyish. The various methods of firing Zulu pots also produce different colours. Dry aloe leaves or wood, and sometimes dry cattle dung, are placed in a bundle on top of a pot ready for firing. Dry grass is put on top of this and set alight. While it is still burning black, more grass is added until it is burning a grey ashy colour, which will make a red pot. To make the pot black, it is placed directly onto the flames of a fire. A firing may last six to eight hours, and some pots are fired twice to obtain different effects. Once the fired pots have cooled, they are often rubbed over with fat and a flat pebble to give them a glossy finish.

The enormous beer pots *(imbiza)* are usually set into the ground and are never moved. Clay basins *(umkhele)* are popular, although in recent times they have largely been replaced by modern plastic or metal versions. Water pots always have a 'neck' or a curved mouth to prevent splashing. Pots similar in size to the pots for drinking beer, but possibly a little smaller, are used for serving *amasi*. Unlike beer pots, these will not have the slip-prevention pattern. Sadly, in many areas today the potter's skill is dying out, as modern aluminium and cast-iron pots replace their beautiful clay equivalents. However, in other areas, potters are producing their wares not only for the local market but also for the ever-growing tourist market.

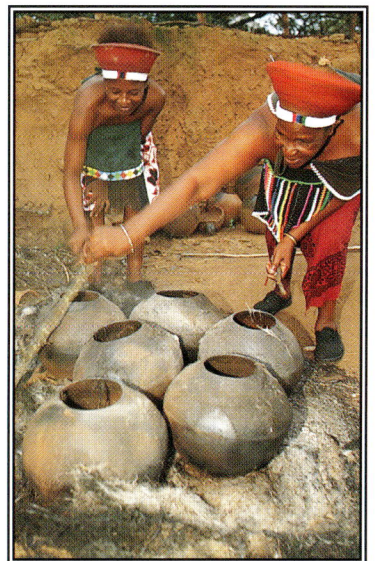

CATTLE

Izinkomo zakithi
Our cattle

'Zulu kaMalandela ngokulandela izinkomo zamanye amadoda!' (Zulu, descendants of Malandela, you have forever followed the cattle of other men!) One of the most famous ways of addressing an audience of Zulu people, this play on words alludes to the Zulu's history as a nation of highly successful cattle raiders. Malandela, whose name means 'the follower', is said to be a progenitor of the Zulu people.

RIGHT: White cattle with black ears or noses have for centuries been the mark of the royal Zulu herd, Inyoni kayiphumuli (the bird never rests).
OPPOSITE: These beautifully marked Zulu cattle would have pride of place in any herd. Sombese Sibiya, who owns them, has a gentle way of training his oxen in a very short space of time, calling or singing to them, and sometimes using older oxen to teach the younger ones.

Cattle symbolism permeates Zulu culture, giving colour to the language and meaning to the lives of the whole community. To the Zulu, cattle are more than beasts of burden which provide life-giving milk and meat: surrounded by cattle, a Zulu man is proud and wealthy, his spiritual and mental well-being secured. In the old days, a man without cattle was practically powerless. Since the introduction of the cash economy, money has by and large replaced cattle in many of its former functions, but livestock still plays a vital role in the lives of the Zulu. Cattle's importance is also partly due to their association with the ancestors (*see* The Metaphysical World, page 140).

In addition to being an indication of wealth and status, cattle traditionally played a significant role in all aspects of Zulu culture – political, economic, social, spiritual and aesthetic. They are still used strategically, in the form of *ilobolo*, to cement bonds of allegiance between lineages and families prior to a wedding (*see* Men, page 76). In the past cattle raiding played a major role in inter-group confrontations across the subcontinent, as well as in battles between black and white. Warriors were rewarded for deeds of bravery with cattle, and cattle fines were exacted for misdemeanours, both of which played a large part in encouraging the cattle-raiding activities.

NGUNI CATTLE

The beautifully coloured Nguni cattle, which are considered South Africa's indigenous cattle, are strongly associated with the Zulu, even though they are not exclusively farmed by them. The earliest records of domestic cattle in Africa date back possibly 7,000 years, when the Sahara was covered in grasslands. Archaeological evidence suggests that, when the Sahara dried out some 4,000 years later, people and their cattle moved into north-east Africa, down the Nagana-free corridor of the Great Rift Valley, through Kenya, Tanzania, Malawi, Zambia and finally into Botswana and Angola. Some of the Nguni-speaking groups and their cattle settled further east and south.

On first encountering Nguni cattle, the early European settlers and many later generations of colonists thought them worthless scrub cattle with few viable economic prospects. This perception persisted into modern times, when the value of Nguni cattle was re-established, and commercial cattle breeders began to realize how well suited Ngunis are to the southern African climatic and environmental conditions. Over the centuries, Zulu pastoralists largely bred their Nguni cattle on the range, where a cow could be serviced by any number of bulls. In the process the gene pool was kept open, and natural selection encouraged the development of progeny which are ideally

TOP: *Nguni cattle, which are fertile, cheap to keep and well adapted to bushveld conditions, are still favoured by the Zulu.*

ABOVE: *In the times of the warrior kings, Zulu men drank from the udder of a royal cow, in a ceremony of loyalty* (ukukleza).

suited to their environment. The absence of human intervention in the breeding process eliminated the type of error which occurred when Friesland cows were selectively bred to enhance their milk production, but in the process developed calving problems. Nguni cows conceive easily and calve without difficulty, largely owing to the shape of their rump and sloping pelvis. Although their calves are small at birth, they are hardy and active. This would have been an advantage in the heyday of cattle raiding, when cattle were herded hastily across vast distances from one *umuzi* to another. As an Nguni bull can service three cows in only ten minutes, it is easy to see why Zulu men like to associate themselves with this virile bull (*see* page 62). Nguni heifers produce progeny earlier than other cattle, making them economically desirable. In addition, they are relatively cheap to keep, they do not require much attention, and they thrive in the bushveld. These days the Zulu farm a large mix of cattle breeds, but wherever possible they still favour their fertile Ngunis.

The most famous herd of Nguni cattle is the Zulu king's royal white herd, the *Inyoni kayiphumuli* (the bird never rests). This name came about because King Shaka's herds were so vast that the oxpeckers and egrets did not stop on one beast, but moved constantly from one to the next. Although Zulu kings owned many types of cattle, the *Inyoni kayiphumuli* is a special herd of solid white cattle, with only black ears, eyes and noses, and black spots by which the individual beasts may be differentiated. In days gone by, only the Zulu king was permitted to own cattle bearing this coloration. All solid white calves that were born in the original kingdom were considered as the property of the king. They were rounded up by his warriors and brought to the royal *umuzi* to join the king's herd. During the times of the great warrior kings, such as Shaka and Cetshwayo, a warrior in training took the oath of allegiance to his king by drinking milk from the udder of one of the king's royal cows, straight into his own mouth. Through this ceremony, which is known as *ukukleza*, the warrior was symbolically feeding directly from his king.

It is estimated that, at the time of Cetshwayo's coronation, the *Inyoni kayiphumuli*, his royal herd of white cattle alone, numbered approximately 12,000 head. Henry Fynn, a young Englishman who was destined for an important place in Shaka's kingdom, reported that, during one of his visits to Shaka's kwaBuluwayo *umuzi*, some 60,000 head of cattle were paraded before his party and the gathered Zulu regiments, in herds of approximately 5,000 each, every herd of uniform colour.

Following the battle of Ulundi between the Zulu and the British in 1879 (*see* History, page 35), the royal herd was confiscated by the British as spoils of war. The British were well aware that, by taking the royal Zulu herd, they would undermine not just the warriors' spirits, but also those of the entire Zulu nation. King Dinuzulu kaCetshwayo later rebuilt the herd, which also fell into the hands of the British, but a small herd survived, wandering around in the bush. Had this not happened, the pure Nguni breed of cattle could have disappeared, and been interbred with European cattle. However, the Natal Parks Board, the provincial conservation body of contemporary KwaZulu-Natal, over a period of time collected whatever pure-bred Nguni cattle they could find, which they used to breed a new herd. Many years later, on 4 June 1989, they presented this herd to the present Zulu monarch, His Majesty King Goodwill Zwelithini.

The 'bird never rests' was finally returned to the hands of the Zulu royal family and a proud tradition was restored.

BELOW: Wearing his folk-art trousers (ibhondwe), *this man checks the chain linking the plough to his oxen.*
BOTTOM: Cattle sales and auctions are an integral part of rural Zulu culture. Although the Nguni is still favoured, many other breeds of cattle also change hands.

THE INFLUENCES OF CATTLE

In the cold pre-dawn of rural KwaZulu-Natal, the cattle touch their noses to the branches of the stockade surrounding the byre, breathing misty air from their warm, wet nostrils. A faint glow seeps into the sky, preceding the coming crisp sunrise. In the umuzi, everything is still quiet. The Zulu call this time of morning Mpondo Zankomo *(the horns of the cattle), when it is just light enough to make out the shape of the cattle's horns.*

The Zulu know, love and revere their cattle in an almost religious way, or as if they were people. A large bull is a very important presence in a Zulu homestead. The image of such a bull standing majestically in the middle of the cattle byre, neck stretched back in a bellow, is strongly linked to the Zulu patriarch and his virility. Bulls often pass a small amount of semen just before they urinate. If a bull does this before the head of the household has urinated in the morning, it is thought that the bull's aura or energy will overshadow that of his master. Consequently a Zulu man should be up and about his *umuzi* early in the morning and should have urinated before his bull does so.

In days gone by, a Zulu man who had no cattle could not marry, since the *ilobolo* (bride wealth) had to be paid in cattle. The head of a household controlled all of its livestock; in order to acquire wives and set up their own homes, all his sons and younger brothers required cattle. The household head wielded considerable power over the future of the young men in his *umuzi*, as he could choose to withhold the cattle needed to pay the *ilobolo*. In the course of the twentieth century it has become increasingly

BELOW: Cattle play a significant role in Zulu society. As a symbol of a family's wealth, they are well looked after. Here the cattle are taken out to graze by young Zulu men at the beginning of the day.

common to use cattle as fines: if, for example, a woman falls pregnant out of wedlock, in order for her name to be 'washed clean', the father of the child must accept responsibility by paying (usually) two head of cattle to the woman's family (*see* page 120).

When the father of the home dies, his bull is sacrificed to take him to his final resting place. It used to be customary for the deceased to be wrapped in the skin of his bull, but this practice has almost fallen away today.

ABOVE: An important duty of Zulu men is to care for the cattle. From an early age, boys accompany their elder brothers into the veld to tend to the family's herd of cattle.

CATTLE SYMBOLISM

Bongani and Mzwake have long been friends and rivals. As small boys, they herded cattle together, and more recently they have been good-naturedly vying for the attentions of a young woman from a nearby umuzi. *Today, they are attending a wedding, and stand with the rest of their community in a rough circle around a pair of stick-fighters. In the centre of the circle, the two young men brandish their sticks, slowly circling each other, each sizing up the other. After a fierce bout of stick-fighting, the youths touch hands as the crowd laughs and claps. Suddenly, Bongani bounds across the circle; stopping directly in front of Mzwake, he slaps his shield with his fighting stick. 'Nansi Inkunzi!' he shouts.*

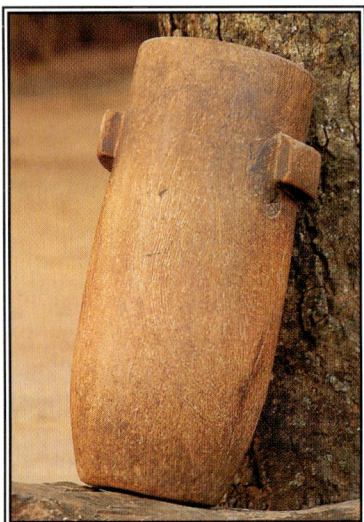

'Here is the bull!' is his challenge. Mzwake hesitates for a split second before smiling and shouting his reply, 'And here is another bull!'. Brandishing his stick above his head, he moves into the centre of the circle to take up the challenge.

Images of virile bulls abound in most aspects of Zulu male interaction, and praise names of important men frequently evoke the spirit and characteristics of a bull. For instance, Prince Gilenja, a patriarch of one of the Biyela groups who have played an important role in Zulu history, has a number of praises. One of them he received in his youthful days as a stick-fighter (*see also* pages 80 and 94 for references to stick-fighting). When challenged to a stick-fight, Gilenja would imitate a bull, pawing at the dust with his feet. He would then rush and butt his head into an anthill, emulating a bull sharpening its horns. Once his opponent was suitably disconcerted, Gilenja would face him with ants and dust streaming down his face. This earned him the praise, 'Gilenja gubha ihlabath, Inkunzi egubha' (Gilenja, the bull who claws at an anthill).

OPPOSITE TOP: *Through the years, Nguni cattle have been interbred with many European breeds.*
OPPOSITE BOTTOM: *The handles on the side of this milk pail stop it from slipping as it is gripped between the knees during milking.*
LEFT: *A Zulu man squats on his haunches to milk his cows, grasping the wooden milk pail between his knees.*
BELOW: *To prevent a cow from kicking during milking, her back legs are tied with a leather thong. She is also tied to a tree or a post to stop her from walking off.*

NAMING CATTLE

Kalazome, a favourite cow in Majola's herd, has a beautiful and melodious low. On a still evening as Majola herds his cattle back to his umuzi, people living close by often hear him calling out Kalazome's praises. As soon as he stops to take a breath, Kalazome bellows her reply. When she stops, Majola continues, and so it goes, each calling the other in the setting sun across the hills, as they meander back to the cattle stockade. The two of them are the cause of much mirth at weddings and beer drinks because of their 'conversations'.

TOP: *Nguni calves are small at birth, but hardy and very mobile.*
SECOND FROM TOP: Incokazi – *a beast with red and white markings.*
SECOND FROM BOTTOM: Inkone emnyma – *mirror-image black.*
ABOVE: Isiphungumangathi– *crowned eagle.*

Cattle are regarded by the Zulu as very intimate and personal belongings. Since they play such an important role in Zulu culture, it is not surprising that cattle are given individual names and that the Zulu often develop close relationships with their cows, even designing praises for them. A good herdsman will not only know the names of all his cattle, but will even be familiar with their lineage.

Cattle are frequently named after significant occurrences that take place within a community. Their names can be regarded as a 'walking history' of a particular family, a constant reminder of some event. A beast may be called *Kalazome* (cry, but the tears

BELOW: A herd of Nguni cattle graze in the rolling hills of rural KwaZulu-Natal.

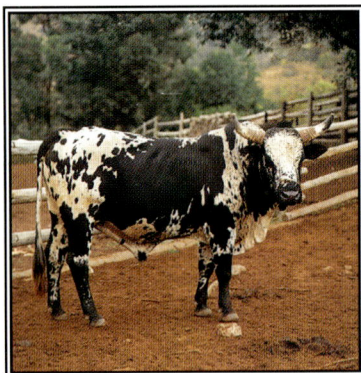

BELOW: Nguni calves are small at birth, but very hardy.
BOTTOM: The distinctive markings of a beast of the royal herd (Inyoni kayiphumuli): mainly white, with black markings.

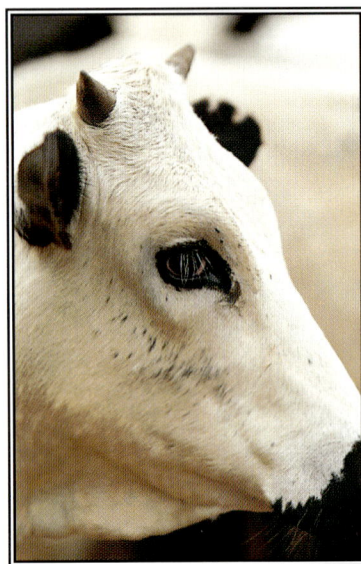

In the Nguni cattle register, Bert Schroeder explains there are six basic colours: white, black, brown, red, dun and yellow, with mixed colours more common than solid colours.

emhlophe – white
emnyama – black
ensundu – brown
ebomvu – red
emdaka – dun
empofu – yellow

eventually dry up), which means that, although things may be going badly for you at the moment, eventually everything will be rectified or solved. Another name may be *Ziyanyunda* (the girls are speaking badly of me), which could refer to an unfortunate or embarrassing occurrence in the life of a young herdsman, when the girls of his community were gossiping about him behind his back.

A black cow with white on the underside of her belly and down the inside of her legs, which resembles the underside of a ground hornbill when it takes off, is called just that: *Insingizi isuka.* Another jocular name for a cow with black and white markings may be *Abafazi bewela umfula* (woman crossing a river), because the pattern is said to resemble a woman lifting her skirts as she crosses the river. The shape of the horns also gives rise to some beautifully descriptive names. The name *Abafazi bepika icala* (woman denying a court case) may be given to a cow with horns that go straight up, like a woman throwing her hands up in court saying, 'It is not me!'

NGUNI COLOUR-PATTERNS

Xolani proudly brings the cattle home at night. He and his brothers and male cousins have been herding the family's cattle since they were small boys. Xolani cannot count but, as the cattle plod through the gates of the stockade each evening, he knows exactly which beasts, if any, are missing. As a child, Xolani was trained to recognize the colour-patterns of the cattle, and particularly of those in his charge. He knows each of the cows by sight and name, precluding the need to count them. In fact, in Zulu culture, it is considered improper to count the cattle.

The names given to groups of cattle with similar colour-patterns are quite different from those given to individual cattle. Over a hundred Nguni colour-patterns have been recorded in Zulu linguistics and culture. No two beasts have exactly the same colour-pattern, which researchers consider the most recognizable manifestation of the gene diversity of Nguni cattle.

The Zulu people have given Nguni colour-patterns delightful names which frequently evoke their environment and culture. In 1992, Bert Schroeder, an ardent enthusiast and expert on Nguni cattle, recorded the colour variations and names of cattle in an extensive register. He says: 'When the Nguni migrations reached "old Zululand" they discovered a paradise with an incredible diversity of beautiful animals, reptiles, trees, flowers and grasses. To each they gave imaginative, yet very apt and descriptive names. These names they also applied as praise names to their cattle. Owning a herd of uniform colour, particularly one of the sought-after colours, added enormously to the status of the herd and to its owner.'

Colour-pattern names may also be praise names which, as they often reinforce and eulogize human characteristics, indicate the attributes which are favoured by the Zulu people. Because of this, these names help in understanding Zulu culture. For instance, the dun and white *inkone engumhlangwe* pattern resembles the skin of a file snake, a creature which the Zulu regard with great awe and respect. The phenomenal rise to power of the Zulu nation, as a result of their military prowess, can be attributed to traits such as courage, bravery and morale; to the Zulu, the file snake epitomizes these qualities. In spite of being a shy and non-venomous snake, it is a great predator of other highly poisonous and aggressive snakes, for instance the spitting cobra. The appellation *inkone engumhlangwe* is thus not given merely to the colour-pattern, but is also used in praise of valour. Any dun and white *inkone* in a herd would be given the special

praise name *umhlangwe*, and a herd sire of that particular colour-pattern was esteemed. The sought-after *inkone* pattern has a 'mirror image' of white on the back and on the belly, separated by a panel of colour.

The *Inyoni kayiphumuli* are the distinguished solid white-coloured cattle most favoured by the Royal House of Shaka. The Swazi, who are another branch of the Nguni-speakers, were as proud of their cattle as their Zulu counterparts, and black was the dignified colour of the royal Swazi herd *(umbala omnyama)*. The Khumalos of the Ndebele kingdom were the greatest cattle raiders of all time. They could not resist the flashy colours of the *inkone ebomvu*, the red 'mirror-image' pattern. *Inkonekazi eyiviyo* is the name in praise of a very popular, vitamin-rich fruit, the wild medlar fruit. A beast of this conspicuous sour-plum colour-pattern added grace and visual impact to a herd.

The *inkwazi* (fish eagle) represents regularity and orderliness, as symbolized by the fish eagle. Dawn in rural KwaZulu-Natal is heralded by fish eagles, which are most vocal at this time of day. Herdboys are awakened early every morning by this clear, evocative call of Africa, which summons them to lead their cattle to pasture.

Other colour-pattern names include: *amaqanda kawayiba* (eggs of the spotted dikkop); *inkonekazi engamaqanda kahuye* (speckled like a bird's egg); *inkanku* (Jacobin cuckoo); and *inkone engamafu* (the mirror image with clouds).

ABOVE: Cattle are often given individual names, and a good Zulu herdsman will know the names of his entire herd.

MEN

Nazi izinkunzi
Here are the bulls

Rebuking a Zulu man in
public undermines him.
His pride, his very identity,
is linked to maintaining his
status as an authoritative
figure: as head of his
household, brave fighter,
father, provider and
protector of his domain.
A man who challenges
a Zulu in a way that
belittles him may be met
with stony silence and icy
dignity, or he may find
himself facing an angry
stick-fighter.

*RIGHT: The skin used in the
head-dress of a Zulu warrior
indicates his regiment. In the
past, seeds or wood were used in
beadwork, instead of the glass or
plastic that is prevalent today.*
*OPPOSITE: Vayisi Biyela, of the
ruling Biyela lineage, wears a
leopard collar* (amambatha)
and headring (umqhele), *with
cow tails hanging from his elbows
and the side of his front piece*
(isinene). *The* izinjobo *(tails)
of the* isinene *move on the thighs,
giving a man a ceremonial stride.*

Traditional Zulu society is a strongly patriarchal one, and many of its cultural practices are geared towards maintaining a man's status as the undisputed head of his household (*umnumzane*) and a figure of authority. Sensitive to misrepresentation of the terms in which he would like to be perceived, a Zulu man will be quick to defend any real or imaginary slight to his dignity. Modern influences, such as the increasing economic independence of Zulu women and the Western education that is available to their children, are slowly changing the way in which the men are perceived. However, to a certain extent, the ethos of the Zulu man, defender of king and country, hunter, lover, and brave and undaunted free spirit, still lives on in rural KwaZulu-Natal.

Zulu men traditionally drew many of their behavioural patterns from the animal world in which they lived, and in which many still live today. At weddings and other ceremonies where groups of men gather, the imagery used by men in their war songs and chants likens them not only to virile bulls, but also to powerful wild animals such as lions and elephants. In so doing, they project the qualities of these animals onto their own characters and lives. In other African cultures, men may relate to the emblems (or totems) of a wide variety of animals, for instance a jackal, porcupine, monkey or fish. Zulu men feel that a direct, powerful approach, such as being identified with a bull or a lion, better represents the ideal character to which a man should aspire.

During a stick-fighting challenge, a man will call out, 'Nansi inkunzi' (Here is the bull), to which his opponent will respond, 'And here is another bull'. A bull is seen as an individual, standing on its own, with its own power. This is how Zulu men like to be seen, especially during the fiercely individualistic activity of stick-fighting, when he pits himself against his opponent.

When a man takes part in a ceremonial dance with a group, however, he will refer to himself as an ox rather than a bull, because inspanned oxen work as a team, all pulling a plough or a wagon together for a common purpose. Similarly, as part of the dance team, a man must have perfect timing, dancing in unison with the rest of his group and, on occasions such as these, he willingly subjugates his individualism for the good of the whole group. This mental shift in attitude, accompanied by a corresponding shift in the imagery and language used to describe the ceremony, by and large characterizes Zulu men: fierce individuals for the most part, but able to work together for the common good when the circumstances call for it.

BOYS

Since the age of five, Sipho and his two cousins have spent their days watching over the cattle as they meander through the bush, grazing here and there, before moving on. Early one morning the three boys get up earlier than normal and, instead of herding the cattle to the appointed grazing place, they take them over the hills, and finally hide them in the forest in a deep valley. They are gone the whole day, and do not return that night. For a while after the sun has set, Sipho's father, brothers and uncles wait in vain for the cattle to return to the umuzi. *The older men realize that the boys are letting them know, through this abduction of the family's cattle, that they are becoming men.*

Unlike a girl's rites of passage or *icece* (*see* page 115), Zulu boys do not go through any specific ceremony to mark the transition from boyhood to manhood, and they do not undergo circumcision. It is rather a gradual evolutionary process, marked by subtle changes indicating that they are growing up. The few 'rituals' which do take place may be initiated by the boys themselves, when they believe adults should start treating them as men rather than as children. For example, the boys will rise early one morning and abduct their father's cattle from the cattle enclosure. They will herd them to an inaccessible place where they believe they are in a good position to repel anyone who tries to retrieve the cattle. Herdboys will undertake such a foolhardy mission only when they feel they have a strong chance at holding the cattle for a period of time. This is a signal to the older members of the family that the boys believe they have reached an age where they can participate in the predominantly male council meetings *(ibandla)*.

Another subtle signal that a boy is growing up is when, instead of calling him to eat from the communal bowl with all the other young boys, one of his sisters brings him his own individual plate of food, serving him in the polite fashion that women adopt

BELOW: *Young boys begin to learn stick-fighting skills during their days as cattle herders.*

ABOVE: The carefree time of boyhood are marked by days playing in the fields and rivers of rural KwaZulu-Natal.

towards men. She may even serve him in the extremely polite *hlonipha* fashion of respect, going down on her knees as she would do for someone of importance (*see also* page 23). This will take place after his sisters and the other women of the *umuzi* have watched him to see how he is behaving; if they feel that he is beginning to show maturity and a sense of responsibility, they will indicate this to him and to the other members of their community in various ways. By serving him separately from the other boys, his sister is showing that he has 'arrived'. His father and brothers may then concur, and it will be agreed that he can move out of the common-room or dormitory which he shares with the other younger boys, and his own home (*ilawu*) will be built especially for him. His sisters will help him to decorate it with beautiful pieces of cloth or craft work. This becomes the young man's lair, where he can entertain friends in private.

Once he has his own *ilawu*, a young man will begin courting. Wearing fashionable clothes which display his physique, he will spend a great deal of time down at the river with his friends, trying to impress a particular woman, so that she will send him the beads of betrothal, *ucu* (*see* page 119). For young Zulu men, the affirmation of their peer group is extremely important. While group activities are the order of the day as they grow up, it becomes equally important for them to receive the affirmation of women. Because of this, much time and energy is spent courting young women and

attempting to prove their prowess as lovers. Young men usually have strong and close relationships with their mothers and, strangely enough, are often encouraged by their mothers to engage in many sexual conquests. It would appear that women obtain some status from their sons' being considered popular and successful lovers.

The day a young man receives the betrothal beads is a proud day for him. Even though he may already be treated as a man, until he can prove that he intends settling down and becoming a responsible member of society by marrying, he is not really accepted as such. As long as he is single, a Zulu man is considered a social light-weight. While a bachelor, he may be allowed to attend, and even address, the council. However, until he has a home and family of his own, he will not be taken seriously by the older, married men. He must also prove that he can raise the *ilobolo* (bride wealth) necessary to marry. Then the rest of his community will consider him a responsible person who is committed to the institutions of society. All these provide important incentives for a young man to start acquiring cattle and establishing himself.

Zulu men are not circumcised to mark their transition into manhood, unlike men in many other South African groups, such as the SeSotho and the Xhosa. This practice was abandoned even before Shaka's time, when in the late eighteenth century the passage to manhood was marked by promotion into one of Dingiswayo's age-grade regiments, rather than by circumcision. Zulu men have a great need for recognition of their particular status in life; one of the ways in which this is achieved is by incorporating young men into 'age regiments'. All young men of a similar age, regardless of geographical place of origin, are formed into a regiment. Even if a man has no other status within the community, in his age regiment he will always be linked to other successful men or

RIGHT: *Zulu boys are encouraged to be loyal, brave and chivalrous, qualities that are highly respected within the Zulu community. These boys are from the Dludla home at a place called Ncayini.*
OPPOSITE: *A young Zulu man proudly wears his* umqhele *(headband) which signifies that he is a man of some status in his community.*

to the overall success of the regiment. Within their regiments, men are thus accorded respect and treated with decorum, and are greatly affronted when they are not treated appropriately. These age (as opposed to geographical) regiments assisted the old warrior kings in preventing the formation of dissident armies which could take up arms against the monarchy. In modern times the continuing existence of these age regiments could possibly also explain the relative ease with which, in periods of political or industrial unrest in cities, Zulu leaders are able to galvanize warriors into action.

In traditional society, it is believed that, as a man matures, the hardships meted out to him strengthen his character, providing him with the experience he needs to teach those younger than himself. Older men are respected and their authority is not questioned unnecessarily. However, urban society is essentially driven by the power of youth which does not have the same reverence for age. As a result of this, the position of the Zulu man is to a certain extent being undermined in the urban environment.

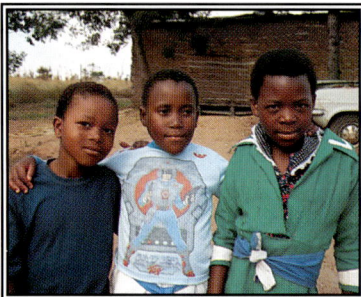

BELOW, MIDDLE AND BOTTOM:
The tasks which defined Zulu men in the past are slowly being replaced and altered by modern education, sport, and other urban Western influences.

BRIDE WEALTH NEGOTIATIONS

Under normal circumstances, when the emissaries of the prospective groom arrive at the bride's parents' house for the bride wealth negotiations, they call out, 'We have come to request an ember of light from your fire'. However, on this occasion, the polite form of approach will not do, because the young woman is already pregnant. Ntombela and Barry approach with some trepidation, and tentatively call out, 'The dog has already eaten the cooking fat'. At this, the old women of the house rush out and begin whipping the men, who beat a hasty retreat, calling placatory remarks and apologies over their shoulders. They stop a safe distance away, and wait for the women to calm down and call them into the stony atmosphere of the home, to begin discussions.

Bride wealth negotiations are quite an ordeal, and a young groom-to-be never meets with his in-laws directly to negotiate the *ilobolo*, or bride wealth. This is always done by emissaries of his family, or trusted friends, so that, if anything should go wrong with the negotiations, it will not sully the relationship between the young couple or between the groom-to-be and his in-laws. Negotiations are even trickier if the bride-to-be is already pregnant. The expression 'The dog has already eaten the cooking fat' indicates that things have happened out of the correct sequence. In such a case, the people negotiating on behalf of the young man are at a distinct disadvantage. In the past, a Zulu woman would have been expected to bear at least one child before the bride wealth was exchanged in full, as proof of her fertility, but these days, with the influence of Christian values and morals on traditional Zulu practices, the situation is quite different.

Marrying is an extremely expensive business for a young man. Before the *ilobolo* negotiations can begin, the groom has to give clothes, money and other items to the sisterhood to which the object of his attentions belongs (*see* Women, page 110), and he may have to buy his prospective mother-in-law blankets or other gifts. He would most likely also have had to pay money towards his bride's coming of age ceremony (*see* Women, page 115), and towards the 'gifts' the sisterhood brings when they deliver the betrothal beads to him. If the bride is pregnant before the wedding, such as in the case described above, the young man will be required to pay a hefty fine in cattle.

In the past, the *ilobolo* was comprised entirely of cattle. These days, especially in urban areas, cash equivalents are more common, and sometimes large items (refrigerators or stoves) may change hands. This is frowned upon by traditionalists, who believe that goods or cash do not provide long-term security for a growing family: cattle breed and

ABOVE: Ngcingci, who sometimes works at Simunye Cultural Village, teaches a young boy the finer points of stick-throwing.

increase in value, but cash can be spent foolishly and commodities depreciate with age. The amount of the bride wealth is often dictated by the status of the family of the bride-to-be, as well as the perceived wealth of the groom. The greater the girl's status and, increasingly these days, the higher her level of education, the more head of cattle will be asked by her father. In the event that a girl is pregnant before the bride wealth has been negotiated, a fine of one or two beasts will be added to the total. Although the cost involved in paying *ilobolo* can be quite heavy, it is more or less balanced by the dowry which the bride takes with her to her new home.

Negotiations can be complex and lengthy affairs. Before the girl's father will begin discussions, money often has to be paid up front by the groom's emissaries. Fathers claim the reason for this is to ascertain how serious the men are, and whether they are in a financial position to negotiate. During negotiations, the number of head of cattle will be decided (although the cash equivalent may be paid rather than actual beasts), and also the preferred colours. In the case where Ntombela and Barry were acting as emissaries of Zinja who had made the girl pregnant, they had to pay quite a bit to show they were serious, and to make her father's 'teeth chatter' (to make him talk to them).

ABOVE: Young men dressed in their traditional dancing attire. Dancing reaffirms a Zulu man's masculinity, his camaraderie with members of his own age set, and his sense of affinity with his history.

RIGHT: Ngcingci goes to the river to meet Nozipho. The rules of chivalry are stressed during the years of courtship. Young men will dress in fashionable outfits that best display their muscles while they are courting girls down at the river.

OPPOSITE: Many young Zulu men aspire to being a maverick and skilled stick-fighter.

CHIVALRY AND COURAGE

In Zulu society, chivalry is one of the marks of a man. To people from other cultures, the extremes to which Zulu men took, and sometimes still take, the rules of chivalry, may seem foolish and difficult to understand. For example, two young men may be vying for the attentions of one girl. Should they both arrive at the river to court her at the same time, neither will in any way try to denigrate or obstruct his rival, as may happen in another culture, since this would be considered to be the worst form of foul play. At all times, the rivals will be courteous and even quite jocular with each other, accepting the spirit of 'May the best man win'. Should one of the men insult or imply anything improper about his rival, the girl would take it as a sign of extreme bad manners. The young man would find it very difficult to continue with this courtship, and he might even find that he had jeopardized his chances of success in future courtships.

In the past, if a warrior were wounded in battle, his wife, sister or lover would often throw herself over him in the heat of the battle. No warrior from a neighbouring group would strike her or attempt to pull her away in order to dispatch the wounded opponent. With this action, the man was protected and his life saved. Zulu people have an enormous respect for courage and chivalrous behaviour, and a woman who undertook such a brave action would be honoured by the enemy warriors, who would leave her be, protecting her man with her body. Obviously, this type of bravery is no longer prevalent, especially not during the violent uprisings that have occurred in the urban areas, but in traditional society it used to be very much the order of the day.

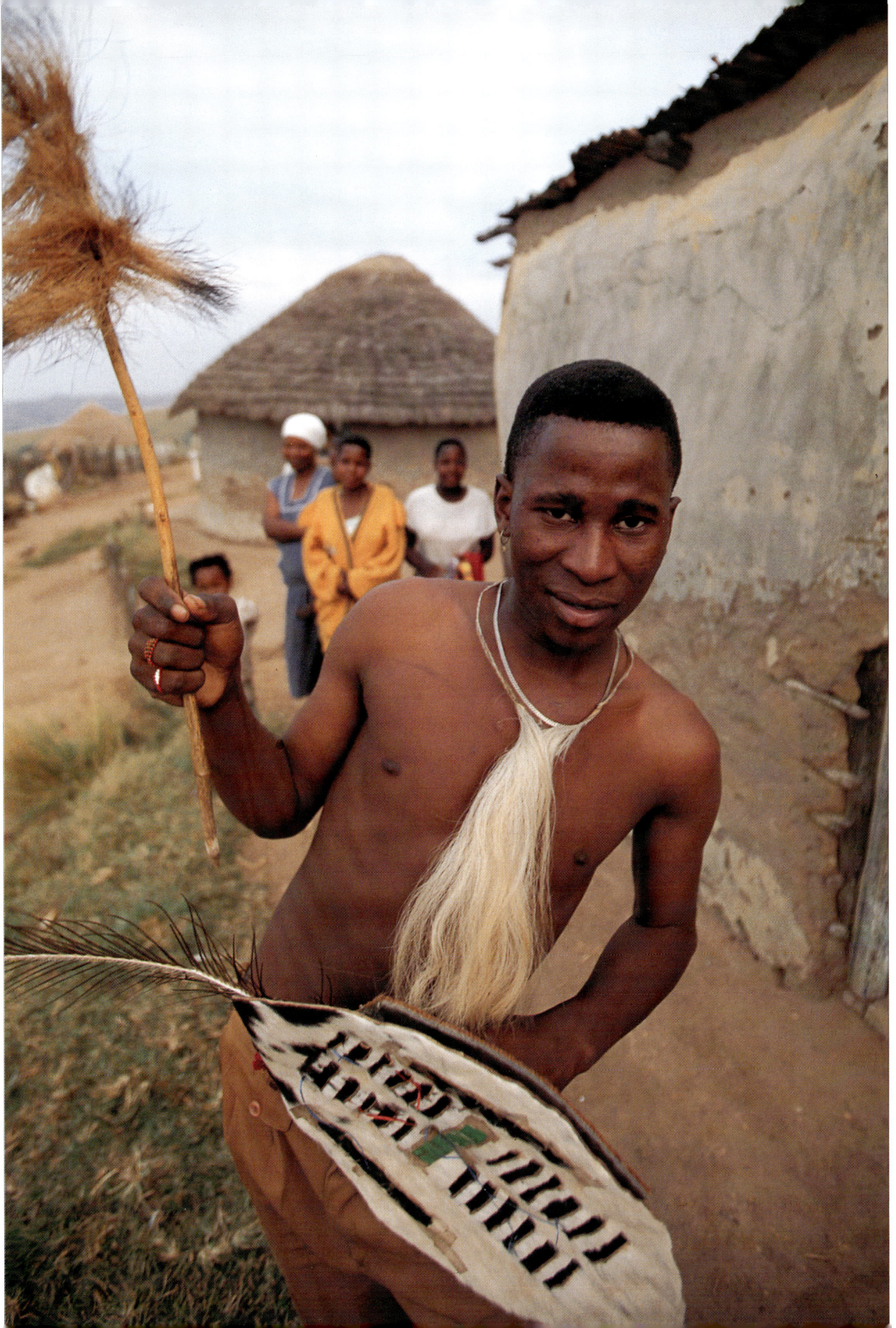

To an outsider stick-fighting may look violent, but to many Zulu it is a celebration of manhood. Although it has been equated with the martial arts, in reality stick-fighting is still developing as a fighting art form, and has yet to be officially recognized as such. The skills required for a man to be acknowledged as a good stick-fighter are learnt through a long process of practising and watching others fight. Their prowess is tested and refined over many years of challenging and fighting others, mostly at weddings, where stick-fighting challenges take place.

Stick-fighting has three main applications: through it men may redress a wrong or an insult; they may practise it for sport, pitting themselves against their opponents in order to prove their skill and manliness; or they may do it for self-defence or as part of a blood feud. In the last case, this is frequently a fight in which both men aim to injure, and sometimes even kill, their opponent. However, there are specific rules of etiquette surrounding the first two applications, for instance a man may fight only against someone from his own age set, a man may not strike an opponent who has lost his stick or who has surrendered, and only sticks are allowed.

Boys traditionally began learning to stick-fight at the age of five or six. While this may seem very young, the herdboys needed to be able to protect themselves and their cattle from wild predators. They also needed to be able to fight other young boys who attempted to 'steal' the good grazing areas, and they might even be called upon to help defend their families. So their training was undertaken in earnest, and was not just for fun, although obviously the boys often enjoyed themselves in the process.

The older boys in charge of teaching the youngsters would tease and mock the boys a little, but they would also keep their eyes open for any boy showing talent. The small boys were given branches of a special switch, which would sting but not do any real harm when it came into contact with their bare skin. This method of training, using branches from the same tree, has been passed down through the ages and is still practised today. The younger boys would be taken far off into the hills where the cattle were grazing; the reason for this was to prevent the ones who were hurt during training from running home to their mothers. Today, as in the past, the ability to stand their ground and not run is as important to Zulu men as their fighting skills.

The Zulu greatly admire courage, especially in the face of unequal odds and danger. This quality was nurtured by King Shaka, and ultimately helped to meld the disparate Zulu groups into a great nation and formidable military force. Today, if young boys get hurt 'playing' at stick-fighting and start crying, provided that they jump up and try to carry on, their older brothers may tease them a bit, but they will encourage the little ones, giving them tips and showing genuine affection. This gives the younger boys a sense of importance and belonging, which ultimately is essential in building their confidence. On the other hand, if a boy runs off crying, his brothers will catch him and beat him for being a coward, thereby instilling in him the do-or-die ethic so valued by Zulu people throughout the ages.

When a boy turns 15 or 16, the men in his family take him into the forest to find his own set of sticks. During these occasions, the boy may be taught something about the trees and other plants found in the forest, the excursion often becoming something of a mystical experience for the youngster. Having the support and backing of his family is important to a young Zulu man when he participates in stick-fighting, and part of the purpose of the trip into the forest is to prepare the boys both mentally and spiritually. The Zulu believe a man must not go into a stick-fight with 'darkness hanging over him': he must have clear, uncluttered concentration to be able to focus and win a battle.

BELOW: Young men wait at a wedding for stick-fighting to begin.
BOTTOM: Weddings are one of the main occasions when young men have an opportunity to hone their stick-fighting skills.

Being a good stick-fighter has always been considered an enormous asset in a family. With no official police force to speak of in a number of KwaZulu-Natal's more rural areas, a family had to be able to provide a measure of protection for themselves. One theory put forward by the Zulu people themselves, to explain why stick-fighting has not disappeared in modern times, is that for many years, under the apartheid regime, black South Africans were not allowed to own or carry firearms of any sort. In order to protect themselves, they needed another form of defence; for the Zulu, stick-fighting was the obvious choice. Every Zulu man believes that, at some time or another, he may have to account for himself physically. Even the more sophisticated urban Zulu man will know how to use stick-fighting weapons, and he will never go anywhere, particularly out of his own neighbourhood, without his set of sticks. When a migrant worker is travelling, he will frequently carry a small, fairly innocuous-looking stick and an umbrella with him. If he is attacked or challenged, these two items will become formidable weapons in his hands. Some umbrellas have a sharp point on one end and a heavy handle on the other, making them the perfect substitute for a traditional stick.

It is considered most chivalrous for a Zulu man to fight his own battles. However, if a migrant labourer is insulted by someone at his rural home, taking time off work to

ABOVE: *Madaka waves his sticks above his head. During an ukugiya (traditional dance), Zulu men use their traditional weapons to display their skills.*

travel hundreds of kilometres to settle the score in person could cause him to lose his job. Consequently, someone else may undertake to stick-fight on his behalf. A man may also stand in for his younger, weaker or less experienced brother in a stick-fight, which is also considered quite acceptable.

Strict rules of etiquette govern a sporting contest. It is bad form for a man just to rush in with flailing sticks at the start of a fight. The two men must square up against each other. Beating their shields with their sticks, they call out, 'Here is the bull', and then the fight begins. Warrior captains (*see* page 93) usually control a fight, but spectators will intervene if they think the behaviour of either participant unfair. Should a man lose his stick during a bout, it would be unchivalrous for his opponent to take advantage of his temporary handicap. This would also be taken as a sign that he does not have confidence in his own abilities. The fight stops until both men are re-armed and ready. If a man turns his back and walks away from a fight, he knows that his opponent will not touch him. In fact, if his opponent does continue to fight, there will be howls of derision from the spectators, and the warrior captains will intervene and discipline the man. Once the captain separates the fighters, it is against all the rules to continue.

Fights may be arranged between large groups of men, which are a sporting means of practising one's skills as much as an opportunity to prove oneself as a man. These fair fights (impi yamanqanu) between opposing regiments may include as many as 400 men. Although many may sustain an injury – even breaking bones – during the fight, the object is not to kill anyone. Following an impi yamanqanu, the men will help to dress the wounds of their opponents, in order to show there is no lasting animosity.

This type of chivalry, where a strong opponent is honoured, has a historic precedent in the Battle of Rorke's Drift (see page 34): it is said that the Zulu, having failed to dislodge the British, rallied for one last time. According to folklore, this was a means of paying tribute to their enemies for their courage, after which the Zulu then withdrew.

BELOW: Being an accomplished stick-fighter is an integral part of Zulu manhood. The women dance while the men face each other prior to beginning the actual fight.
FOLLOWING PAGES: Two young Zulu men practising their stick-fighting skills.

A blood feud is quite different from an *impi yamanqanu*, and other traditional weapons, such as spears and battle axes, may be used. In a fair fight, only ordinary fighting sticks are allowed. If other weapons are introduced, this usually signals that the fight is going to turn into a full-scale battle.

Shaka was responsible for revolutionizing warfare in the Zulu kingdom, through the introduction of formation fighting and a large shield. When used by warriors in formation, this shield protected and covered the fighters on both flanks. The traditional throwing spear, which had been used up until Shaka's time, was shortened into a broad stabbing spear; instead of standing far off hurling spears at their enemies, the warriors moved in close to engage them in hand-to-hand combat. Through these changes to accepted warfare the Zulu achieved formidable military success.

The making of shields and spears came to be a craft requiring immense skill, since the warriors' lives were dependent on their weapons. Zama Gcugcwa is well known in Zulu society as a man with a special skill for making spears. He had the ability to look at a stone and tell, from the surrounding clay, the quality of the iron within it. The blacksmiths at the time of the warrior kings were often figures to be feared and revered. Having learnt their skill, they would frequently remove themselves from society and lead solitary lives in remote areas close to where the iron ore could be found. This reclusive existence led to rumours that blacksmiths were connected to witchcraft. In the process of forging spears, many people believed the blacksmiths used human fat, but it was not thought that they were directly involved in killing people to obtain it.

Few modern Zulu people are familiar with the traditional skills of a blacksmith, and access to many historical iron-ore deposits has been cut off, because they are situated within proclaimed game reserves. Metalsmiths today use scrap metal when they find it difficult to obtain metal from other sources, even cutting pieces of metal from bridges.

The traditional method of making the metal part of the spear is to place clay containing the metal into a small, very hot fire. The fire is built on a slope so that, when the metal smelts, it will run into a ridge which has been made to mould the metal. Once it has cooled and solidified, the metal is shaped and sharpened using a stone *(mlalazi)*.

Making a spear involves more than just a knowledge of forging metal: the shaft is as important as the metal tip. The shaft needs to be well weighted and strong, so that it does not break, and branches from the *ilala nyathi* (sleeping buffalo tree) are favoured. An iron spike is heated to make a hole on the end of the shaft. *Ingcino* (gum) from the *umsululu* tree is pushed inside the hole, into which the metal spike is inserted. When the gum is dry, strips of cow hide are wound tightly around the end of the spear to hold the spike in place, preventing it from slipping out during fighting.

Traditionally, a Zulu man was not supposed to carry a weapon of war, apart from his sticks, in public *(see also* Sticking-fighting, page 80). A number of different types of spears and axes were used by the Zulu *impis*. The *isijula*, a long throwing spear with a small blade, was used for hunting since the blade does not damage the skins too much. Traditionally only married men were allowed to carry the *isijula* because unmarried men were not considered responsible members of society. The fighting spear used prior to Shaka's time had a medium-sized blade; it was called the *isipapa* because of the sound it made when flying through the air (a rapid 'pah-pah-pah'). This spear was no longer a very effective weapon after the introduction of Shaka's short stabbing spear, the *iklwa*, but is still used as a hunting spear. Like *isipapa*, this name is onomatopoeic, derived from the sound the spear makes as it is stabbed into and pulled out of a man's body ('eengh' as the blade goes in, and 'klwa' as it is pulled out). A large knob at the

THIS PAGE, OPPOSITE AND FOLLOWING PAGES: Making a good spear is almost a forgotten craft these days. The spear-maker prepares the shaft by burning a hole with a hot stake before the blade is inserted. The blade is sharpened on a special stone. This craft has been handed down through generations to Goboti, one of the few spear-makers who are still able to make the large-bladed, short-shafted stabbing spear (iklwa) *that was introduced by Shaka.*

back end of the *iklwa* stopped it from slipping when it was wet with blood; the knob also served as a counter-balance to the heavier metal blade, preventing the spear from being wrenched from the warrior's hand during battle. The battle axe or *isizenze* was used mainly by commoners to push, grab and gash. The swallow-tailed axe *(isisila senkonjane)* was carried only by royalty and used to control their warriors during a battle.

OPPOSITE TOP, MIDDLE AND *OPPOSITE TOP, MIDDLE AND BOTTOM: Men may make their own shields from carefully pre-pared cattle hide. In the past each regiment used to have its own distinctively coloured shields. LEFT AND BELOW: During serious blood battles large shields were used to protect the warrior's entire body, while smaller shields are still used today during stick-fighting or dancing.*

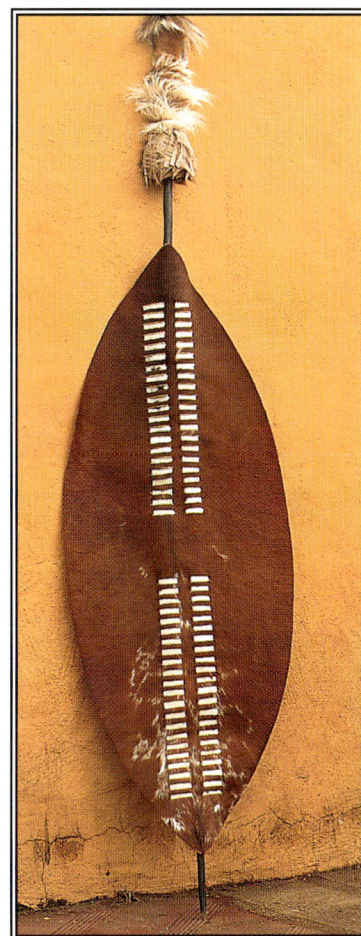

Shields also form part of military regalia. Small shields are used for ceremonial purposes and for stick-fighting, while large shields are used for dancing, or training for war. Dance shields are used as drums, with the dancers punctuating their movements with blows to their shields with dancing sticks. A large shield may be used to conceal weapons and, by holding their shields horizontally while running across the hills, a

regiment of warriors can easily be mistaken for a herd of cattle on the move. During Shaka's time, veteran warriors – those of 35 and older – carried pure white shields. The new, least experienced, conscripts carried pitch-black shields. As the warriors progressed through the ranks, they were allowed to display more white in their shields. In the past many men used to make their own shields, but these days they are usually bought or made by a friend.

In order to make a shield, the skin of an Nguni cow, while it is still wet, is stretched to its fullest capacity and sun-dried. When it is quite dry, the shapes for the shields are cut from it, starting with the biggest shield. Great care is taken over how the shield is cut out of the hide, so that the Nguni pattern of the beast is incorporated on the shield into an artistic design. Next a diagonal line *(amagabela)* is cut in the skin, through which a piece of contrasting hide is inserted, adding to the overall pattern. The final step is to work the handle into the back of the shield.

MEN AT WEDDINGS

There is still a strong military flavour to a Zulu wedding, one of the few occasions when stick-fighting takes place in a more or less official capacity. Men travel 30 kilometres (20 miles) or more to attend a wedding and try out their stick-fighting skills.

Often before a marriage all the men in the district come together, a short distance from where the wedding is to be held, at a gathering of the regiments. This is the forum where disputes are settled and animosity is sorted out. Once this has been done, the warrior captains lead all the regiments to the wedding, the men singing rousing songs with military nuances or chanting war songs.

Just before sundown on the first day of a wedding, the men remove themselves a short distance from the rest of the party, and begin the stick-fighting. Women dance, and men perform the *ukugiya* (*see* page 134). Dancing has a military as well as celebratory application: through dancing, men learn to follow a leader, to keep in step with a group and not to let them down. Many old battles are also enacted through dance.

WARRIOR CAPTAINS

Generally warrior captains attain their position and status as a result of their leadership abilities and the strength of their personalities. A powerful character is necessary to be able to control and contain a regiment of angry young Zulu men. In times of peace the role of a warrior captain is to oversee and discipline the regiments, particularly at ceremonies such as weddings and stick-fighting challenges.

Warrior captains all have their own style, some favouring blood feuds and others fair fights. During an outbreak of political violence in KwaZulu-Natal, an argument broke out between two neighbouring areas. This rapidly escalated beyond stick-fighting into open warfare, in which semi-automatic weapons were employed, and the stage was set for a classic blood feud. At this time, a very humble, but famous and popular, warrior captain, Mgedeni Shoba (*see* picture, page 92), stepped in. Such was his reputation and stature in both of the communities involved that, by appealing to the men's basic humanity and chivalry, he was single-handedly able to diffuse the explosive situation, engineer a cease-fire, and persuade the men to hand their weapons over to the police. Although a small man, he put himself at enormous personal risk to bring an initially unpopular, but lasting, peace to this area.

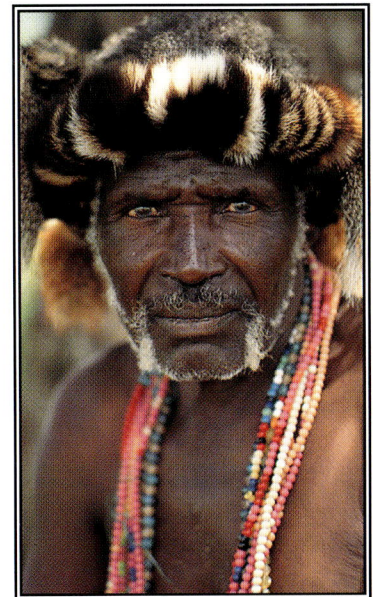

OPPOSITE: *The respected warrior captain Mgedeni Shoba, with his ornately painted fighting sticks, is famous among the Zulu. During a particularly bloody faction fight, Shoba, with his remarkable leadership abilities, managed to defuse a volatile situation and bring peace back into the area known as Hlophekhulu (the big white mountain) by evoking the spirit and ideals of Zulu chivalry and manhood.*

ABOVE: *An elderly Zulu man, Mthimkhulu, whose name means 'big tree', wears a head-dress which normally indicates a man of some status within the group.*

WAR MEDICINES
AND WITCHCRAFT

War medicines, which have always been used before warriors go off to fight, are usually administered by an *inyanga* (herbalist), as opposed to an *isangoma* (diviner) (*see* The Metaphysical World, page 140). It is well known that, during the Anglo-Zulu war of 1879, medicines were used in the belief that they would turn the bullets of the British into water. Similar medicine is still used today by the *impis* before they head off to fight.

The purpose of the medicine *impi kayiboni* is to blind the enemy army so that they will not be able to see the approaching Zulu *impi*. The night before a battle, the men retire into the mountains or forests to prepare themselves, using a variety of medicines. War medicine has another application today: instead of preparing warriors for battle, it is used by sportsmen before a big game, such as soccer.

THIS PAGE AND OPPOSITE: Many Zulu men, who have had to go to the cities to find work, have adapted their rural way of life and their traditional dress to urban circumstances. Others find employment in the game reserves of the province of KwaZulu-Natal in which they live.

MAVERICKS

Sikhakhane, a shabby-looking figure in his tattered clothes, strides up to the group of men happily sitting around, sharing a pot of beer. After he has greeted everyone, he is offered a sip. Having drunk the beer, he leans over and, with his ubhoko *(stabbing stick), pokes an enormous hole through the pot, spilling the beer all over the ground. There is a murmur of disapproval from the gathered men, whereupon Sikhakhane says, 'If anyone doesn't like it, I am available for a challenge.' No-one moves. Some time later, the men come across Sikhakhane lying dishevelled in the path. 'Look at that,' says one of the men, 'a famous stick-fighter, lying quite drunk on the side of the road.' At this the very sober Sikhakhane leaps up, shouting to the unfortunate, startled speaker, 'I take that as a direct challenge. Now you must fight me!'*

Today, as in the past, the self-styled, independent radicals or mavericks *(amashinga)* are a fascinating group of men in Zulu society. While ordinary young men will usually stick-fight as a social pastime, as a way of impressing young women, or as a means of displaying their manhood, a maverick lives for stick-fighting. Usually, although not always, a young man, a maverick will travel great distances, often through hostile territories, to attend a wedding where he knows he will have a chance to challenge a worthy rival to a bout of stick-fighting. He may never have met this man before, but he may know of him by reputation. Defeating this formidable opponent will enhance the maverick's own name as a stick-fighter.

Many mavericks acquire a certain renown in their communities because of their extreme tenacity in a fight and because they are tremendously committed to their fighting. Once they become well known in an area, however, not many men are prepared to challenge them, because they are quite likely to be letting themselves in for a sound drubbing. As a result, famous mavericks do not have many opportunities to put their skills to the test, and so they sometimes have to go to great lengths, like Sikhakhane, to provoke or trick men into fighting them.

A Zulu maverick will frequently dress himself in rather worn and tattered clothes, as opposed to his more carefully and colourfully dressed peers, who may be more interested in courting young women than in the more manly pursuit of stick-fighting. The maverick will make no attempt to spruce himself up, showing a measure of contempt for his 'softer' brothers: by dressing like a vagabond, he makes it quite plain that, after all, his business is fighting, not loving.

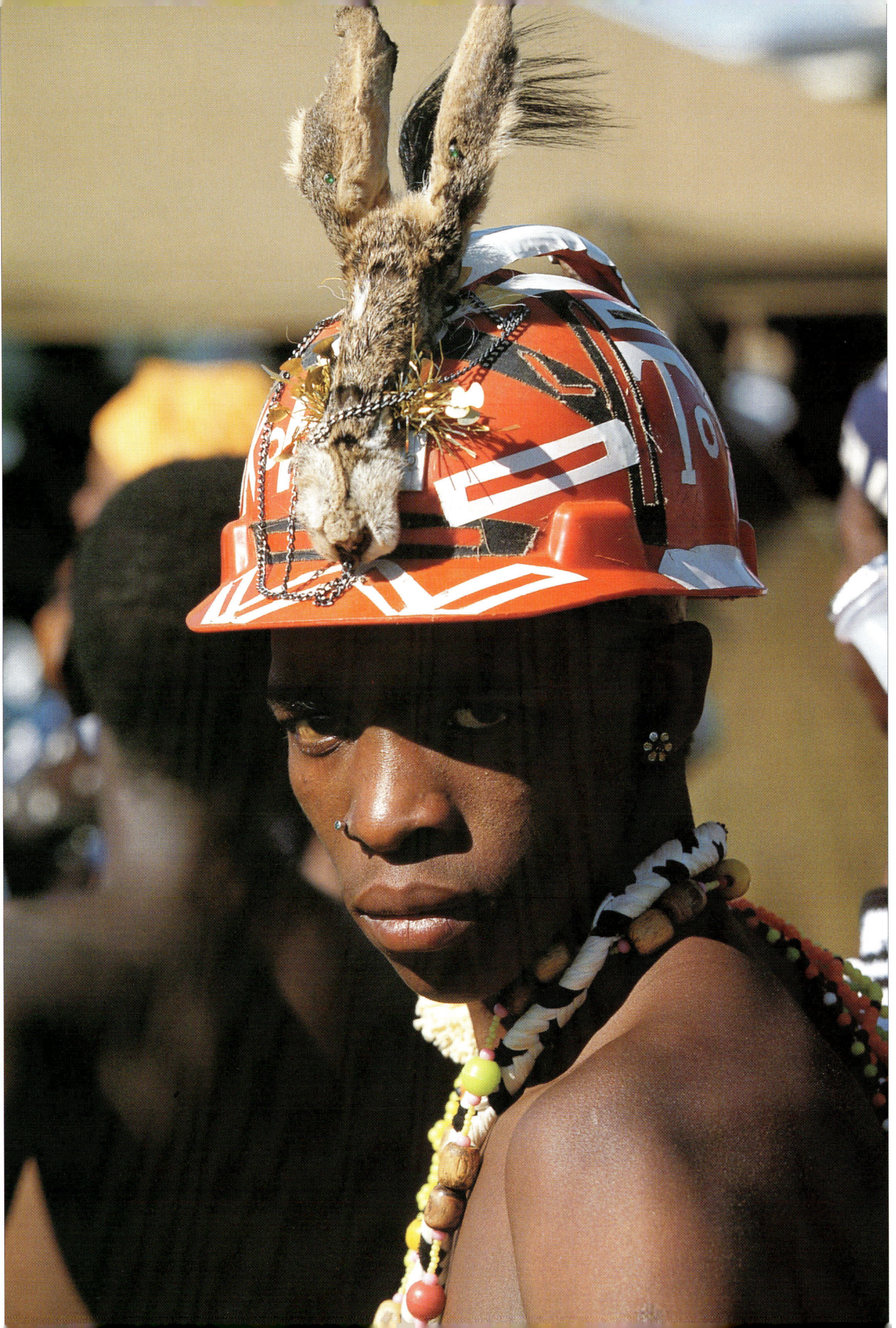

WOMEN

Wathinta umfazi wathinta imbokodo
Strike a woman and you strike a rock

The emancipation of African women is currently a hotly debated subject, but this has had little effect on traditional Zulu people. Rural women live in much the same way as they have for centuries. Yet, despite being classed as perpetual minors, they are not as powerless as many people believe: within the cultural practices which may seem restrictive to Westerners, Zulu women have empowered themselves in their own ways that are not always understood by outsiders.

RIGHT: *Zulu women today play a significant role in maintaining traditional culture.*

OPPOSITE: *The headgear worn by married Zulu women is not as common as it was in the past, although in many rural areas of KwaZulu-Natal it is worn as a sign of a woman's marital status.*

When the sun rises over the purple hills at dawn in the deep rural areas of KwaZulu-Natal, the Zulu women are already up and working, and they frequently carry on working until well after the sun has set. Part of their days are filled with domestic chores: tidying and cleaning their homes, tending to their children, collecting water, washing clothes and ensuring that there is a supply of fire-wood. Later on, they go down to the fields with their neighbours to tend to their crops of maize, pumpkins, ground nuts, beans and sweet potatoes. They return home later to prepare the meals for the family. Some women also find the time in their busy day to do beadwork and make mats and clothing by hand.

In addition to their routine domestic duties, many Zulu women living in towns and cities hold down full-time jobs and are often the sole income-earners in their families. Despite these responsibilities, Zulu women continue to be regarded as minors, more so in rural areas, where traditional practices are more rigidly enforced, than in urban areas. In modern times, changes are being wrought by the process of urbanization and South Africa's new constitution, which accords equal rights to people of both sexes. Many women, both urban and rural, are becoming increasingly economically independent, and some of the traditional practices which constrained women in the past are being challenged. But, by and large, ordinary Zulu women are still treated as minors, and many of the traditional practices persist.

Traditional Zulu society is strongly patriarchal. Strict social rules govern women's behaviour, and it is a brave or stupid woman who defies accepted norms. From early childhood, girls are taught to defer to men and to show them the utmost respect. A girl has to abide by the rules and regulations set down by her father who, as undisputed head of the *umuzi*, has the final say in his household. As an adult, she is similarly bound by decisions made by her husband if she is married, or her father or a male relative if she is single.

It is sometimes mistakenly thought that Zulu women do not own, or have rights to, possessions of their own. Many women do in fact own goats, and a married woman may even own cattle, which are called *izinkomo zesixanu* (the cattle of the maternity belt). These cattle have usually been given to a woman by her father at the time of her marriage. Until a woman has had a baby, the only milk she is allowed to drink is from the *izinkomo zesixanu*; after her first child is born, she may drink milk from the cattle in her husband's byre. In terms of the traditional succession rules, the *izinkomo zesixanu* are inherited by a woman's last-born son.

Land is communal, and so may never be owned by any one person. However, the use of land is allocated to married men for their homesteads. A bachelor is never allocated land: no matter what his age, he remains in his parents' extended homestead *(umuzi)* until he is ready to marry and establish his own. Many people believe that this practice rewards the institution of marriage, thereby encouraging a stable community. Land is invariably passed down through the male line. The only land allocated to married women is their agricultural fields, for which they are individually responsible.

THE POWER OF WOMEN

Power, in the political sense, is generally not bestowed upon Zulu women as a right. It is something which a woman may take, and many have done so. The women in Zulu history who have attained positions of power have done so through the sheer strength of their character. In modern times it is more of a formality than a reality that women may not attend the council, much less address it. Women who are recognized within their community as people of strong character and integrity are often requested to attend the council and participate in the proceedings. In fact, in the early 1990s, Dr. Sibongile Zungu was the first woman ever to be appointed a chief following the premature death of her husband.

Historically, there have been many powerful Zulu women. Although King Shaka never married but kept a vast harem, during his reign women played important roles in Zulu society. Shaka's mother, Nandi, had a tremendous influence on the development of the Zulu nation, and Shaka's sister and many of his aunts headed Shaka's powerful military *imizi*. Despite being a woman, Pampata was one of Shaka's closest and most trusted confidants, and is often credited with being more influential than many of Shaka's male councillors. Shaka also instituted a military regiment to which all young women belonged. Although it never took part in active warfare, it played a significant part in the rise of the Zulu nation.

On the whole, living within the confines of a male-dominated society, Zulu women have learnt the value of creating an aura of power about them, and have developed methods, both individually and collectively, of taking some control over their own lives and of influencing their communities.

MAIDENS

From the time that they are *amantombazane* (little girls), Zulu females have domestic chores thrust upon them. Their younger brothers and sisters and other small children, who may be only four or five years of age, are left in the care of girls frequently not much older than the children in their charge. As the girls mature, they find themselves entrusted with an increasing number of responsibilities.

On reaching puberty, a girl is known as a *tshitshi* (maiden). During this period of her life, a *tshitshi* living in a rural area will go bare-breasted with her head uncovered, thus indicating her single status. In Zulu culture the head is sacred and, when a girl becomes a *tshitshi*, no man may touch her on her head. In modern society, an engaged woman will cover her hair with a hairnet, and a married woman, particularly in rural areas, will never appear in public without some type of head covering, such as a cloth bound about her head, a beret, a hat or, in the case of traditionalists, a head-dress.

Zulu women have long been aware of the importance of being recognized from an early age as industrious and of good character, in order to have the pick of eligible bachelors and make a good marriage. In days gone by, Zulu men were often away from home for long periods of time, when they were staying at their military barracks, fighting wars or hunting. They wanted to be assured that, while they were away, their wives would remain faithful to them and take good care of their families. Therefore, when seeking a marriage partner, they would look for a woman whom they considered to be of steadfast character, and strong enough to resist temptation.

Although for modern urban women the circumstances have changed, a similar situation persists in rural areas. Zulu men still spend long periods away from home: while their forefathers lived in military *imizi* training for war, hunting or going about the countryside fighting and raiding cattle, the cities are often the only places where men can find work today. As migrant labourers in the big urban centres or on the mines, their contracts often allow them to visit their rural homes and families only once or twice a year at Christmas and Easter. So they still favour women who will care for the family and be faithful. A woman who is perceived as lazy, or likely to run around with other men during their absence, will have considerably less chance of marrying well.

Marrying well brings status and a measure of power in her community to a Zulu woman. Because of this, a *tshitshi* will fiercely defend her reputation. She will go to great lengths to feign indifference towards men who court her, behaving in an off-hand and cutting manner, and forcefully rejecting a man who tries to touch her. A mindful

TOP AND ABOVE: *Married women always keep their heads covered in public, indicating their marital status. Traditionalists today still wear a head-dress and a leather shirt* (isidwaba)*. An engaged girl may have her head partially covered by a hairnet, a headband or a traditional head adornment. Covering of the head also has* hlonipha *implications.*

tshitshi holds herself aloof, no matter how attractive she finds a man, or how outrageously he flirts with her. She thus protects her good name as someone who is inaccessible, untouchable and pure. In the past, this behaviour encouraged sexual restraint. During Dingane's time, women could, and did, walk around practically naked, wearing only a string of beads around their waists, with perhaps a small decorative frontispiece. Such was the moral fibre of the society at that time that, even dressed in this way, a woman would be totally secure from any form of harassment or abduction. These days, however, teenage pregnancies have increased to the point where they are the cause of much concern to the Zulu community. The Reed Ceremony, which aims to promote pride in virginity, was introduced in 1984, partly in an attempt to curb promiscuity.

Although she holds herself aloof from young men, a *tshitshi* must be extremely polite and submissive towards other members of the community, particularly those older than herself. Zulu women learn to speak a language of politeness, which, in some areas of the country, is quite distinct from day-to-day conversation. For instance, out of politeness, a woman will not refer to a person directly by his name, especially in the case of senior male relatives, either living or dead. Because of the symbolic and extremely sexual connotations between Zulu men and their virile Nguni bulls, a woman will not use the usual term *izinkomo* when referring to a bull. Instead she will use *inzetha*, which is the polite *(hlonipha)* version. Likewise, a cockerel will be referred to as *impande* – little scratcher, an obvious allusion to a chicken scratching around in the dust – rather than calling it the common term for chicken, *inkuku*.

When a girl becomes engaged she is allowed a degree of latitude in her behaviour, and a blind eye will be turned to slightly aberrant behaviour. Even then her domestic duties do not decrease, and her – usually – minor acts of rebellion and independence are allowed only until she is properly married.

BELOW: Young single women form sisterhoods, all dressing similarly when attending ceremonies or festivities, thus indicating to which sisterhood they belong.
OPPOSITE: A hard-working wife of strong character and good morals is considered a great asset within the Zulu community.

BEADWORK

The most ancient form of beadwork known to have been made by the Zulu were *iziqu* (medallions of war). This necklace, made from interlocking wooden beads, was worn criss-crossed across the shoulders, as a symbol of bravery by warriors. Throughout the period of the independent Zulu kingdom, warriors continued to wear *iziqu*. The beads were hand-carved from indigenous hardwoods such as tamboti. Before glass beads were available in large quantities in the course of the nineteenth century, men and women wore strings of beads, not only made from wood, but also from seeds and berries, which were sometimes boiled until soft and then threaded with a thorn onto the long sinews taken from the muscles in an ox's back.

OPPOSITE: Galaji, whose name means 'garage', sitting outside her home in rural KwaZulu-Natal doing beaded craftwork.
LEFT: A Zulu woman uses a loom to make amacansi *(reed mats). Batteries or stones are wrapped in plastic and used as weights for the threads.*
BELOW: A detail of a hand-woven grass mat.

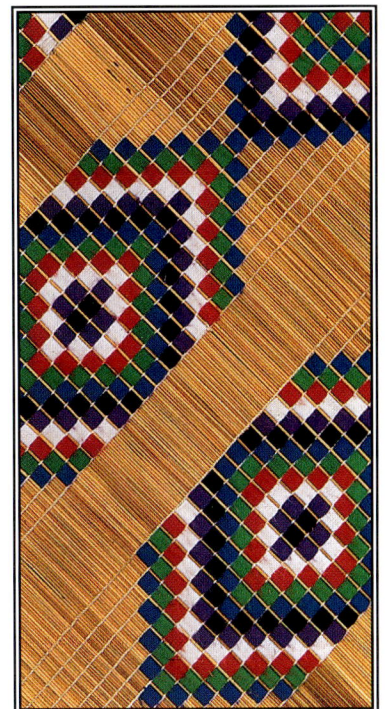

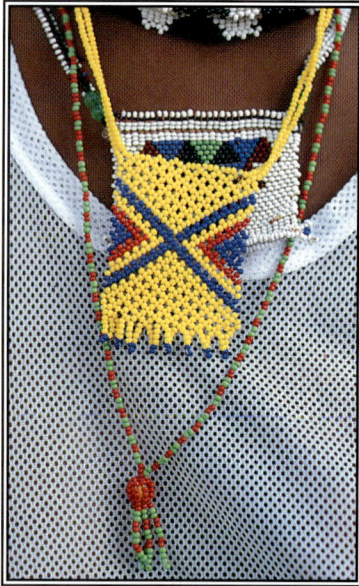

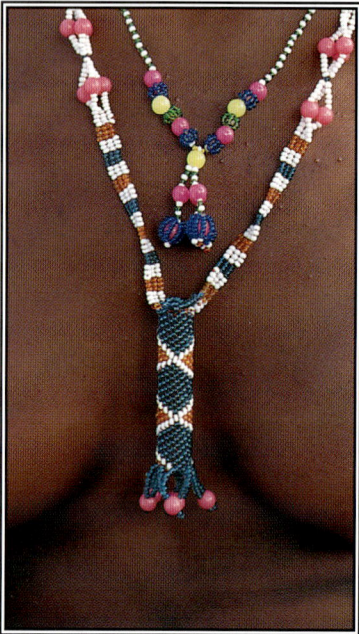

THIS PAGE: *A colourful selection of beaded necklaces made and worn by young Zulu girls.*

THIS PAGE: *These days, modern objects such as beer cans, cool-drink can tops and wool have been incorporated into girls' leg decorations, sometimes replacing the traditional dance rattles.*

ABOVE: *The grass maternity belt* (isixanu) *worn by a married Zulu woman after she has borne a child. This belt lends its name to the cattle of the maternity belt, which are owned by a woman.*

The small, coloured glass beads that are so strongly associated with the Zulu were, as far as can be ascertained, made in eastern Europe and Italy, and introduced to the Zulu by Portuguese traders. Archaeological diggings have found a wide variety of beads which were already being worn during Dingiswayo's time. Before the 1850s glass beads were not as easily available as they later became, with the result that they were initially worn only by the wealthy or privileged.

With the influx of European traders into Africa, glass beads became more plentiful and consequently more accessible to the ordinary people. Although beads were worn by both men and women, they were particularly popular with young unmarried women, who wore long strings of colourful beads wound around their arms and legs, and slung around their bodies.

Teenage girls often make small beaded squares, called *Themba*, which they give to young men with a colour-coded message woven into the design. *Themba* means a combination of promise and hope or trust. In different parts of KwaZulu-Natal, a variety of fashions of beadwork developed with different coloured beads and distinct patterns symbolizing a wide variety of meanings. This discrepancy has sometimes led to confusion and misrepresentation among students of beadwork. For instance, in some areas, green beads represent jealousy, while, in another region, green may represent grass, and carry the message, 'I will wait for you until I am as thin as a blade of grass'. Yellow may be used to symbolize jealousy, white most often represents goodness and purity, and blue stands for loneliness. If black beads are used, especially in the middle of a red square, this may mean that the girl does not love the young man. However, black may also be used to represent the black rafters of a roof, showing that the girl's love is solid and she will wait for her lover. Pink is sometimes used to denote poverty and to convey a sharp message, telling the young man not to waste the girl's time until he has enough cows to pay for the *ilobolo* (bride wealth). Red is for love, and in some areas symbolizes the blood of a bleeding heart.

The *ipasi*, a particular type of beadwork found mostly in the Tugela basin around the Msinga area of KwaZulu-Natal, is a type of choker chain. The word *ipasi* is derived from 'passbook'; during the apartheid years, black people had to carry a passbook with them when they travelled around the country. Once a Zulu man was in possession of a passbook, he was allowed the right to move about the countryside more easily. In the same way, once a young man received the *ipasi* from a young woman, he could take it that he would be allowed certain 'rights'. The *amagaliga* are little beaded anklets, which are also made by a young girl for her lover. Traditionally in certain areas of northern

BELOW: Skirts frequently have messages embroidered onto them, which can be quite pointed in their content. The message on this umbiso, *which is worn by unmarried, post-pubescent girls, means 'Protect me from my enemies'.*

KwaZulu-Natal if a mother discovered that her daughter was making *amagaliga* for a young man of whom she disapproved, she would confiscate the beads and put them around the ankle of one of the household's dogs, to show that she thought the prospective lover was no better than a common dog.

The *isixanu* contains important significance in Zulu culture. It is the maternity belt worn by a woman after the birth of her first child, and symbolizes her transition into full acceptance by her husband's ancestors, since she has borne an heir. This belt lends its name to the cattle which are owned by a married woman, and are not included in the general household paternal herd; these cattle are known as *izinkomo zesixanu* (the cattle of the maternity belt).

ENGAGED WOMEN

Nozipho pulls on her red vest, over which she wears a smart, white, long-sleeved shirt. She rolls up the sleeves just so, and then ties a piece of bright blue cloth over the towel she has wrapped around her waist. She secures it carefully with safety pins. Finally, donning a pair of white, canvas, sand-shoes, she heads down the path to meet her friends, all of whom are wearing outfits identical to her own. The girls make their way across the fields, heading towards a nearby umuzi *where a wedding is being held. Across the hills, a strong voice calls out to them. It is Mzwake, who has been showing an interest in Nozipho for a few months. She lifts her head proudly and ignores him. One of Mzwake's companions calls out again to the girls. This time, one of Nozipho's friends shouts back a withering answer. The young women all burst out laughing – in perfect, mocking unison. Chastened, the young men hurry on their way.*

Young Zulu women of a similar age form peer-groups, or 'sisterhoods', which generally consist of unmarried female friends and relatives from the same geographical region. Collectively, as part of a sisterhood, young women wield more power than they would as individuals, and they use this to ensure they are treated with respect. As *amatshitshi*, young women come under the influence and guidance of these sisterhoods and, with their support, a young woman will seldom be bothered by the unwelcome attentions of any suitor of whom the group disapproves. The women also dress in identical clothes and use similar mannerisms. They may learn to laugh in unison in a derisive fashion, sounding like a flock of hadeda ibis flapping away; the effect of this can be quite disconcerting, which is exactly what the women desire.

Young women who are engaged to be married *(amaqhikiza)* usually enjoy the most influence within a sisterhood, because they are not as restricted as the others. It is commonly accepted by the community that *amaqhikiza* are in transition from one household to another: they are no longer really controlled by their fathers, and yet, until they are officially married, they do not have to comply with their husbands' rules. This is one of the few times in their lives that women are allowed a measure of freedom.

The *amaqhikiza* and the sisterhood, rather than the parents or other adults of the community, closely monitor the behaviour of not only potential lovers, but also the members of the sisterhood. They also orchestrate and advise on relationships between young people. Although an aunt or mother may sometimes have a certain amount of knowledge of a suitor, Zulu parents in general are seldom privy to their children's budding relationships. The girls go to great lengths to keep their fathers completely in the dark about what is going on – until it is time to formalize a relationship with the *ilobolo* or bride wealth negotiations.

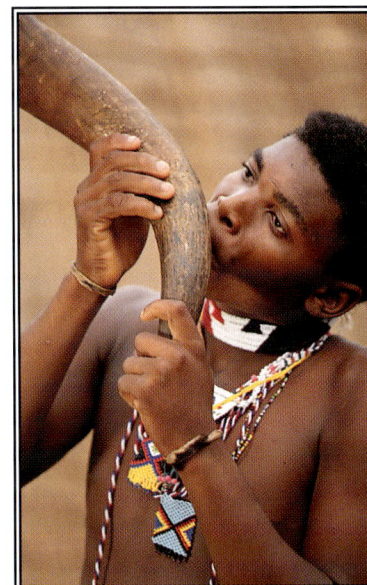

OPPOSITE: *The headband worn by this young Dludla woman indicates that she is betrothed.*
ABOVE: *Mzwake blows on a cow horn, letting everyone in the district know that he has been accepted by a young woman and is now engaged.*

For some months, Sufiso has been courting Danile. Things were going well, until word reached her sisterhood that Sufiso had told his friends he had 'claimed Danile's virginity'. Danile disputes the story vehemently, but it is decided that the only way to discover who is lying is through an age-old method, which has long been used to test the truth. Danile sits on the grass next to the river. Her friends stand around a small open fire, upon which is set a three-legged pot in which they are cooking maize. When the maize is cooked, the girls call Danile. She sits cross-legged in front of them, bracing herself and gritting her teeth. One of the older girls lifts a steaming spoonful of maize from the pot, waits while some of the water drains off, and then suddenly slaps it on the inside of Danile's thigh. In a flash, Danile grabs the maize and puts it into her mouth, her eyes streaming with pain. She quickly swallows the maize, and looks defiantly at her friends. The girls leap about, jubilant. Now they need to find the guilty suitor.

Had Danile obeyed her instinct to brush the hot maize to the ground, instead of whipping it into her mouth, this would have been a sign of her guilt: it would be taken to mean that she had voluntarily given her virginity to Sufiso. However, by scooping the maize into her mouth, she proved her innocence. The girls knew that Sufiso had slandered Danile's good name, and would have to be punished. This method of testing innocence continues in rural KwaZulu-Natal to this day.

BELOW: Every day Zulu girls and young women go down to the river to fill their pots with water.

The sisterhoods take their duties of watching the behaviour of suitors seriously. If the young women feel that any man has stepped out of line, they take action against him. It is quite acceptable for the members of a sisterhood to fine a young man who has affronted one of them. No slight to their honour is tolerated or left unanswered, and an insult to one is considered an insult to all.

If the young women of the sisterhood are outraged and angry enough, and the offence is serious enough, they will march to the culprit's *umuzi*. At the gate of his *umuzi*, they will strip naked. Total nakedness is a terrible social taboo in modern Zulu culture (although this was not the case for unmarried people during the nineteenth century). By stripping, the women emphasize the gravity of the offence. This is also an extremely effective method of focusing the attention of the entire community on the man's misdemeanour. The other residents of the *umuzi* may avert their eyes from the naked women, but it is extremely difficult to avoid noticing such a noisy and unusual scene. Attracting the attention of the entire community is of course the idea and, as far as the women are concerned, it gratifyingly adds to the culprit's humiliation.

ABOVE: The river is a favourite spot for young men to meet and court the Zulu maidens of their choice.

The girls get hold of the young man and he is ordered to bring his 'fine', and meet them down at the river where a ritual ceremony will take place. The fine may be fairly hefty, but it is minimal compared with the humiliation that is suffered by the young man in question. Standing in the water, the women tear the money into little pieces, which they throw into the current. They then bathe in the river, symbolically cleansing themselves of the insult.

COURTSHIP

Mandla calls out to the herdboy, who smiles and waves, before trotting off up the hill to tell his sisters that Mandla is waiting at the river. His sisters send a message back that he should wait until their parents are asleep before approaching the house to meet Zakhone, the object of his affection. The sisters will secretly bring his supper to him at the river, as they have been doing for some months. Because Mandla cannot yet afford the bride wealth (ilobolo), the girls have gone to great lengths to keep him a secret from the rest of the family. On this night, as one of the sisters is preparing to steal away from the house with some chicken for Mandla, her grandfather calls her back. Taking the tray, he orders her to stay in the house. He covers his head with a cloth, such as one of his engaged granddaughters would wear, and makes his way down to the river where Mandla is waiting. Stooping slightly in the respectful manner a young girl would adopt to a man, the old man approaches Mandla, who is hiding in the reeds. Expecting one of Zakhone's sisters, Mandla steps out and starts to thank her. The old man shrugs off the cloth and, whipping a sjambok (a long cattle whip) out from under his arm, beats Mandla across the shoulders, shouting 'I see you have been eating my chickens for some time, but I do not see the bride wealth yet'.

It may take a young man quite some time to be accepted by the young woman whom he would like to marry. In some cases, he may not be able to afford the bride wealth, sometimes he is working in the city and cannot get away to see his beloved all that often, and sometimes he may take so long courting her that she gets tired of waiting for him and chooses another man.

In the early morning all the young women go to the river to collect the household's water, and this is the ideal place for the age-old Zulu courtship traditions to continue. Every day the young women and girls from the *umuzi* hoist their clay pots onto their heads and walk through dewy grass, down the cool, dusty paths to the river, to collect water. The water bubbles over the rocks and rushes along the sandy river banks as the women submerge their pots, rinse them out and fill them with fresh water. While the women are laughing and chatting, standing ankle-deep in the water, young men, dressed up in their courting outfits and carrying their sticks, arrive at the river. A young man will try to impress the chosen *tshitshi* by showering her with compliments, and praising her with riddles and elaborate poems of love. But, regardless of the distance he may have travelled, the reception he receives is likely to be icy. Her sisters may banter with and tease the young man, but the young *tshitshi* herself will studiously give him the cold shoulder. The suitor will have to work hard to break through the girl's defences. Courtship may carry on for several months, or even years, particularly if the young man works in the city and cannot come to the river frequently to meet his sweetheart. When several suitors arrive simultaneously to woo the same young woman, this is generally accepted in good spirits by all of the rivals. Each of them will patiently await his turn to try to impress her.

Top: *Ngcingci on his way to the river, where he hopes to meet Nozipho, the young woman whom he is courting.*
Above and opposite: *Mzwake is also wooing Nozipho at the river. Much teasing and bantering goes on during the courtship rituals, and young men go out of their way to make a favourable impression on the young women.*

Although it may appear that men are the ones who select a mate, the final choice actually lies with women. This places them in a strong position of power. A man has to prove himself before he is accepted by his sweetheart. It is in this selection that the sisterhood often plays a significant role, assisting a *tshitshi* in assessing how serious her suitor may be about marriage. They will consider his prospects, his reputation, his family, how persistent he has been, and how sincere his professions of love are: Does he really mean what he is saying? Does he continue to visit even under difficult circumstances? Is he of good character? Will he provide well for a family? If a young man is particularly lucky he may have a sister or other relatives within the sisterhood, who can forward his case and speak on his behalf to his sweetheart and her family.

COMING OF AGE

On the day of Gugu's icece *(her coming of age ceremony), she is dressed in a traditional cloak. This large cloak, of deep ritual significance, is made from an ox's diaphragm which has been dried and through which a hole has been cut for her to place her head. As she stands in the centre of a group of her friends, her head is covered with money as it is pinned to her hairnet by well-wishers.*

At about the time a young woman is thinking of forming a permanent relationship, she may undergo the *icece* (coming of age ceremony). Today, *icece* often takes place at the same time as a woman's engagement, but this depends on whether her father can afford to pay for a separate ceremony, and on how well she has conducted herself as a *tshitshi*.

Before the ceremony can take place, the young woman is taken into seclusion by the other women of her community. She is isolated from society for up to two months, during which time she is treated as a lady of leisure, kept out of the sun to prevent her skin becoming dry or burning a darker colour, and fed on the best food.

By the time she returns to her community, she should be looking her best: her skin glowing, her eyes bright and her body a little plump (this being considered a sign of health, desirability and beauty). The time in seclusion is not frittered away entirely on making the young woman look attractive. During this period, the secrets of woman-hood are imparted to her, and she is instructed in the duties of becoming a wife, a mother and a respected member of the community. On her return to society, the *icece* is held, announcing to the ancestors and the rest of the community that the young woman has comported herself favourably and is now coming of age. In the course of the *icece*, the young woman's family slaughters an ox from which she obtains a caul of fat which she wears while dancing for the assembled guests. This symbolizes the protection that her ancestors will afford her when she leaves her home in order to marry and live in her new husband's homestead.

On the sloping hillside near to the houses, hundreds of men gather to watch a long string of maidens who slowly begin to dance, all carrying small ceremonial spears. Every now and then, one of the girls, breaking away from the long lines of singing dancers, singles out a man, moves towards him, and finally plants the spear in the ground at his feet, before re-joining the other dancers. After a short while the man gets up and returns the spear to the girl before breaking into a wild war dance, called *ukugiya*, which indicates how honoured he is at being able to participate in the *icece*.

The acknowledged husband-to-be of the young woman may follow tradition and walk, with his family, the long distance from his *umuzi* to hers. His family are expected to make a statement to her community and a meaningful financial contribution to

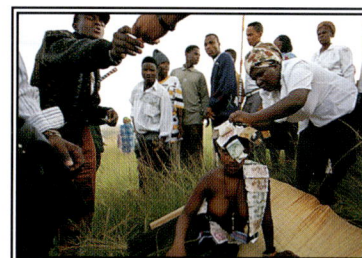

OPPOSITE: The older women in the community gather on the hill-side to watch the dancing during a coming of age ceremony.
TOP: A young man gives a girl a box of matches while she dances. By giving her something which she will have to return to him at the end of the dancing, the young man increases his chances of speaking to her.
ABOVE: Young men pin money to the head of the young woman who is coming of age. In this way the whole community contributes towards her dowry.

ABOVE: Grandmothers no longer have to impress anyone and their often slightly outrageous behaviour is tolerated by the rest of the community. Here an old woman gets up to dance at a coming of age ceremony.

RIGHT: A Zulu girl, her head festooned with bank notes, dances at her coming of age ceremony. She is not wearing the caul of fat normally worn by young women while dancing at their icece ceremony.

OPPOSITE: Recently engaged, this young man proudly wears the white betrothal beads (ucu).

the ceremony. They prepare an *isikhafu* (scarf), onto which so much money has been pinned that it may be difficult to see the colour of the scarf. The friends of the young woman dance up to the group of her betrothed, and kneel at their feet in an act of honour and welcome. The young man and his brothers then put the scarf onto the girl, before they and the guests all move into the houses for an evening of dancing and games. A master of ceremonies is appointed for the evening, and food and drink are

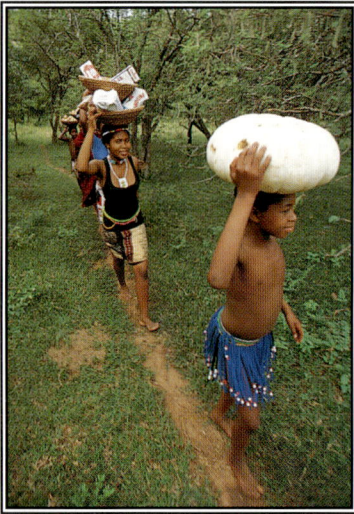

ABOVE AND RIGHT, TOP: The female relatives of a young woman take food and gifts to the dwelling of her future husband to let him know that his suit has been successful.

RIGHT, BOTTOM: As the young man emerges from his dwelling, the girls whip him energetically with thin switches – just to let him know who is really the boss.

OPPOSITE, TOP: Once he has been given the special white betrothal beads (ucu), the young man is teased by the girls, who light-heartedly give him a lesson in personal hygiene.

OPPOSITE, BOTTOM: To thank his bride-to-be for accepting him, the young man holds a special thanking ceremony (umbongo) at night. This ceremony, which takes place far from the parents' homestead, is attended only by the young people.

provided. These refreshments are usually 'sold' at very inflated prices, which the people are happy to pay, since they know they are contributing to the young woman's future welfare. The game *ukushaya indishi* (strike the dish), which is often played at an *icece*, is another way of raising money for the young woman who has come of age. A spirit of one-upmanship frequently develops among the young men, as they challenge each other with outrageous dares. Failure to fulfil the dare means they have to pay a forfeit into the dish. The only way out of the dare is to counter it with an even more outrageous challenge, coupled with an even higher forfeit. As people enter into the spirit of the game, enjoying the food and drink, the dish is 'struck' with piles of money and, by the end of a successful and enjoyable evening, it is stacked high with notes.

CHOOSING A HUSBAND

Once a young woman has decided upon a husband, she needs a way of letting him know that she has accepted his proposal. She sends her sisters to the young man's homestead with a special set of beads, which are called the *ucu*. The girls take gifts of food for his family, as well as 'gifts' for the young man.

When the girls arrive at the young man's house, they knock politely on the door. As he stoops to come through the low doorway, they will lay into him with small switches, whipping him on his arms and legs, laughing as they do so. Once he recovers from his surprise, he will be delighted, because he knows that the whipping precedes the delivery of the *ucu* beads. The act of whipping the young man is a symbolic way of letting him know that, from here on, the sisters will be in charge of the relationship between him and the young woman, and that he had better not step out of line. They then give him his 'gifts': soap, toothpaste, a toothbrush, facecloth, deodorant and a

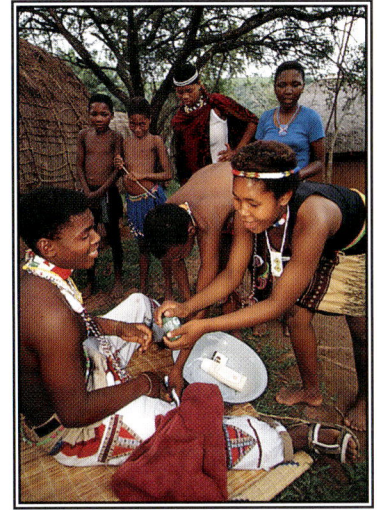

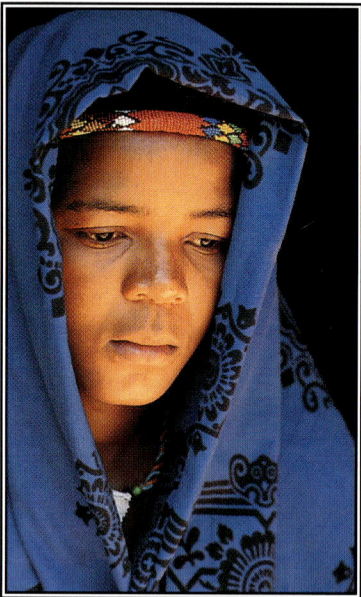

TOP: *To let everyone know that he has become engaged, the young man and his friends raise a tall flag near the cattle byre of his father's home.*

ABOVE AND OPPOSITE: *As a sign of respect to her new husband-to-be and to his friends, Nozipho shields her face during the thanking ceremony, keeping her head covered and eyes lowered in the traditionally subservient* hlonipha *fashion.*

small towel are all unpacked from a large enamel wash basin. The girls pin the young man down and playfully force the toothbrush into his mouth, showing him how to brush his teeth and lecturing him on personal hygiene. In this way, they are telling him he should not think that, now he has been accepted by his sweetheart, he can slacken off – they will be watching him.

The following day, the young man and his brothers and friends raise a long flagpole in the centre of the *umuzi* near the cattle byre. If he was the only suitor, he will raise a white flag to let everyone know he has been accepted. If there was more than one suitor, he will raise both a red and a white flag to announce his success.

Since his sweetheart made the first move by choosing him, it is now his turn to reciprocate, which he does through the ceremony of *umbongo* (the thanking ceremony). But, before this can take place, he has to comply with a number of requests from the sisterhood, to show that he is taking the relationship seriously. He may be required to supply all of them with matching sand-shoes, socks and cardigans, and perhaps blankets for their mother. Once he has managed to acquire all these things, he sends a message to the older girls, requesting that they set aside a time for the *umbongo* ceremony.

In the dead of night, under a tree far from their parents' *imizi*, the young man and his friends will go to meet his betrothed and her sisterhood at the appointed time. This ceremony is, in effect, the engagement ceremony. The newly engaged woman is now required to *hlonipha*, which means she must show all the signs of respect due to men. She covers her head, keeps her eyes downcast and, in a further demure symbolic gesture, even covers her face by holding a small branch of a tree before her. Later, there is much feasting and dancing among the young people.

SEX AND PREGNANCY OUTSIDE MARRIAGE

To this day, some Zulu people still practise *ukuhlobonga*, which is a method of having sexual intercourse without penetration. This traditional practice became popular during Shaka's rule since the king wished to avoid impregnating the women of his harem and the risk of having a son who might kill him. *Ukuhlobonga* has always been considered an acceptable form of sexual activity, even outside of marriage.

However, in the event of an unmarried woman's falling pregnant, the father of the child has to pay a fine in cattle to the woman's family. By acknowledging his paternity and paying the cattle, the man effectively 'washes clean' the young woman's name, and the reputation of the family is restored. The cattle are also a means of providing for the future well-being of the baby. If the man does not acknowledge the child, it will automatically be brought up by the woman's family, and it is possible that he may never come forward to lay claim to it. It sometimes happens that, once the child has reached puberty, the biological father will arrive with the cattle, in which case he can then claim his rights as the child's father.

If an unmarried woman has a baby, and the father does not come forward to claim his child, the mother will often marry another man, which may lead to later confusion. Such a child is commonly kept in the dark about the true identity of his or her real father until just prior to her or his wedding. Since the ancestors play an important part in the social fabric of the Zulu, and no-one can deceive the ancestors, it is considered important that the person be told at some stage who he or she really is. This can be very traumatic. A man could end up being accompanied to his wedding by total strangers, who are actually the family of his biological father, but whom he may never have met in his life before his wedding day.

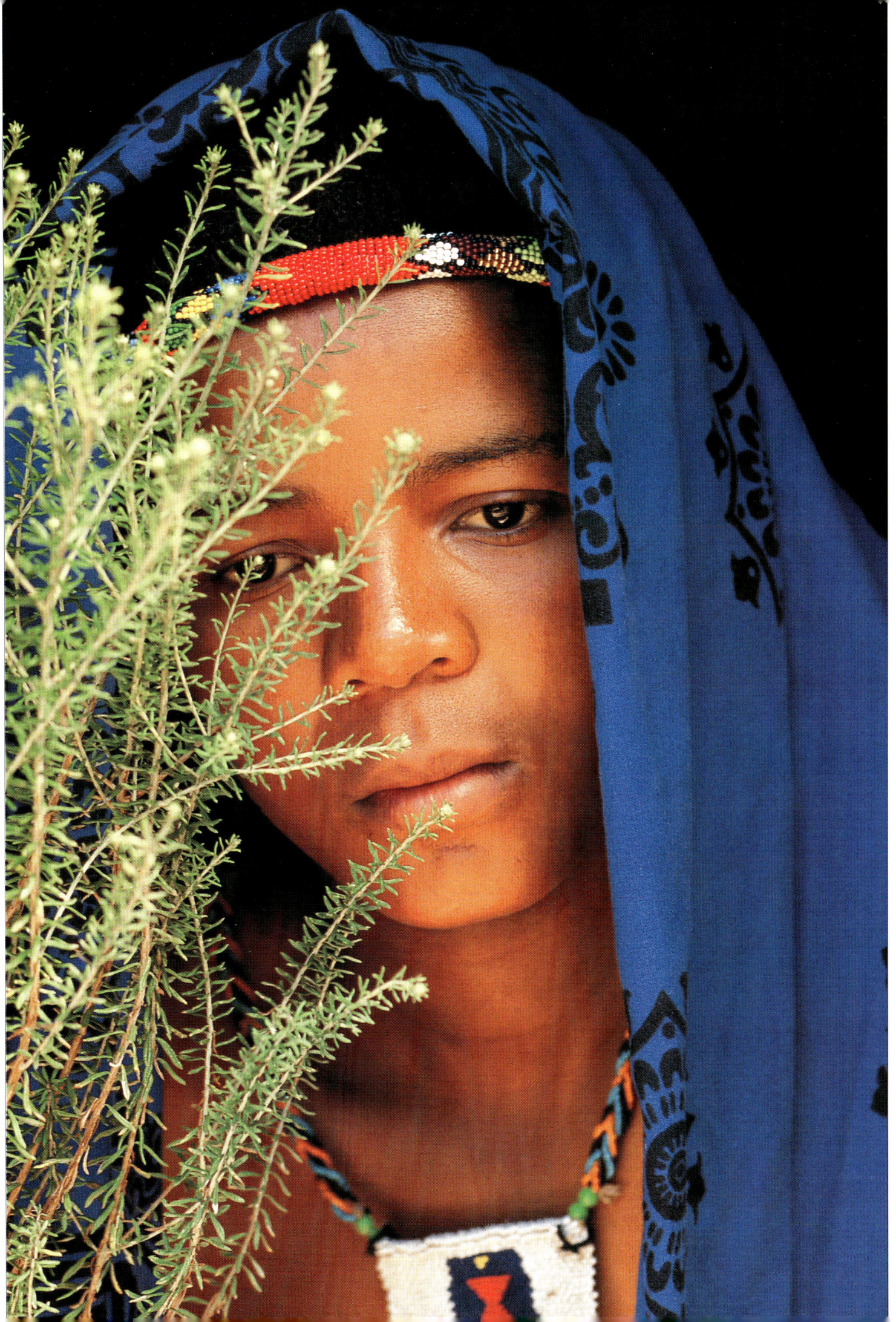

MARRIAGE

Sengathi ningalala nibabili nivuke nibathathu
May you lie down as two and stand up as three

A Zulu wedding is more than just a ceremony formalizing a union. Many serious problems that may arise in a marriage are exposed at the ceremony in a joking manner: through the competition between the two families and the way the people dress; the dancing and the words of songs which are often composed to reveal every deed, good or bad, of the couple and their families. In this way, there are no nasty surprises to be dealt with later in the marriage.

RIGHT: A bugle, possibly a relic from the Anglo-Zulu war, is played by a relative to get people's attention when announcements need to be made at the wedding.
OPPOSITE: Nonhlanhla Shezi with her face covered in the traditional manner of Zulu brides. She carries a spear, shield, black umbrella and lantern, symbols of her transition from a single girl to a married woman.

Negotiations to determine the amount of *ilobolo* (bride wealth) still form the basis of most Zulu weddings (*see also* Men, page 76). Although many rituals and ceremonies precede a wedding, only once agreement on the *ilobolo* has been reached does the engagement become official. The father of the prospective bride will then set the date for the wedding. When Christianity was introduced to south-east Africa, *ilobolo* was equated with the sale of women, and attempts were made to discourage it. However, the practice continues, and many fathers believe that *ilobolo* is more important now than ever before, as a way of ensuring that suitors are fit and capable of providing for their daughters and their daughters' children in these economically difficult times. In addition, it is felt that *ilobolo* compensates the father for the money that he has 'invested' in his daughter over the years, and for the loss of her labour in his *umuzi*. Young men may earn low wages or struggle to find work, and it may take them many years to pay the *ilobolo*. Consequently, the couple often marries before the full bride wealth has been paid, but these days this is not considered ideal. In the past it was usual for the *ilobolo* to be paid in instalments – part payable before the wedding, part after the birth of the first child and so on.

Before the wedding has been formalized with the exchange of the *ilobolo* cattle, gifts are given and cattle need to be slaughtered at different stages throughout the courting ceremonies, the preparations for the wedding, and during the marriage proceedings themselves. This means that a Zulu wedding is an expensive affair for both of the families involved, as well as for their friends.

As soon as the date for the wedding has been set, the family of the bride informs all of their friends and relatives that their daughter is going to be married. The young woman visits these people and receives little gifts (*ukucimela*) from each of them. *Ukucimela* is derived from the word *ukucima* (a candle has been blown out), the gifts symbolizing the leaving behind of the old life (blowing it out) and the starting of a new life in a new home. People usually give the bride something small that she can use in her new life, such as a basket, a little pot or some money.

Even though the wedding ceremony is usually held at the *umuzi* of the groom's father, many preparations first need to be made at the *umuzi* of the father of the bride. Her family slaughters one of their cattle in the cattle byre, in order to announce to the girl's ancestors that she will soon be leaving her childhood home and going to join the ancestors of her new husband.

The day before she leaves her father's home, the young bride accompanies her father on a walk through the cattle byre to say farewell to the cattle and to her ancestors. Finally, the night before the actual wedding ceremony takes place, the bride sets off on

foot for the groom's home, accompanied by her immediate family, other relatives, and friends. If the groom's family live quite far away, the bride and her entourage will leave early in the evening before the wedding day and walk right through the night. If his home is not too far off, they will leave home at about midnight or in the early hours of the morning, in order to arrive before sunrise. The young woman walks away from her childhood home naked, covered only in a blanket, symbolically leaving everything of her old life behind. No matter how far they have to walk, everything the bride's father has bought for her and all the gifts that have been given as part of her trousseau, are carried by the family to the bride's new home. This may entail carrying wardrobes, beds, kists, chairs and tables, baskets and mats across the hills.

The night before the wedding, neither the bride's party nor the groom's family will get much sleep. The former have to walk most of the night, while the latter usually have an all-night party. Even though all his friends are celebrating, the groom is not allowed to do much work or dance too much. Instead, he sits on the side-lines while the older men in his family give him advice about marriage, work and life in general, spurred on by jovial interjections from his younger friends. The bride's entourage arrives while it is still dark, and sets up camp under a tree outside the groom's father's *umuzi*, a custom known as *esihlahleni*.

THE PARTY BEGINS

In the cold morning air, Gugu and her family sit huddled in blankets in their camp under the tree as the sun begins to rise. Two of her uncles, her elder brother and some male cousins pull their coats around them and make their way towards the umuzi *of Vincent, Gugu's husband-to-be. As the party approaches the entrance to the* umuzi, *dogs begin to bark and a group of people rush out of their homes shouting and laughing. With long poles, Vincent's sisters and cousins try to prevent the visitors from gaining entrance to the* umuzi, *but finally, singing, yelling and laughing, the new-comers force their way in.*

An element of competition between the parties of the bride and groom is an important part of a Zulu wedding. A fierce, but always good-natured, contest is held to establish which group can put on the more exciting display of dancing, or be the more colourful, spirited and entertaining. The competitiveness starts early in the day, as the bride's male relatives approach the *umuzi* of the groom. Some of the groom's friends and family attempt to stop them at the gate, and young girls rush out with long sticks to try to bar their way. But the bride's people are inevitably allowed to force their way in, accompanied by rowdy merriment and singing.

Having gained entrance, the bride's party breaks into a special dance (*ukugqubushela*), which prompts the rest of the groom's people to rush out of their homes and start a dance of their own. The two parties, both men and women together, face each other in two long lines and start to dance energetically, leaping up in the air, crouching down to the ground and whirling around kicking their legs and waving their arms, singing and laughing as they stamp their feet. Eventually one of the groups, unable to keep up with the frenetic pace of dancing, will lag and back off. If the bride's people are defeated, they will be chased out of the *umuzi* but, if they win, they return victorious to their camp under the tree. From this point on, throughout the morning, emissaries from the groom's *umuzi* will go down to the bride's people under their tree to welcome them and serve them tea and coffee. More often than not, a goat will be sent down to their camp to be slaughtered.

THE WEDDING CEREMONY

At a Zulu wedding there is no set order of events or master of ceremonies to organize the proceedings. A councillor or family elder is the only person who might play some sort of official part. Usually a comical fellow, who will frequently appear decked out in a World War II uniform or parts borrowed from other uniforms, his function is more that of a policeman – to keep the peace and monitor the revellers – than that of an organizer of actual events. As it happens, the whole group happily stumbles through the events of the day.

In the early afternoon of the first day of the wedding, the bridal party makes their way towards the *esigcawini*, a sacred ceremonial place just outside the groom's home, where they are met by the groom's people. The bridal party takes up a position at a bottom of the slightly sloping ground, and the groom's party will stand at the top.

A second series of dances begins, some of which have been specially choreographed for the occasion. The young women from the party of the bride dance to the ancient *inkondlo*, which is a type of family anthem. The young men from the groom's party go down and hand personal items to a dancing girl of their choice, having singled her out as a good dancer. This provides an opportunity for them to meet and talk to the young women who, according to custom, are expected to return these items to the men once the dance is over.

TOP LEFT: *Sleeping mats, on which the bridal couple and other important members of the family will lie during the wedding, are spread out on the grass.*
ABOVE: *The men of the groom's party sit on the hill watching the dancing.*
TOP RIGHT: *While they are engaged, young women enjoy considerable freedom from the constraints normally placed on women.*
OPPOSITE: *The trousseau, which may consist of beds, kists and household linen, is carried from the bride's home to the groom's home, where the wedding will be held. The bride sits quietly, dressed in a leopard skin outfit, while the groom's family dances a little way off.*

At some undesignated point in the wedding proceedings, the bride's father and a small delegation of men from her family will announce to the people gathered that all is well and the bride wealth has been paid in full. If this is not the case, they will state exactly what is still outstanding, so that there can be no later misunderstandings to mar relations between the couple or their families.

An important part of any traditional Zulu ceremony is the saying of praises *(izibongo),* acknowledging the ancestors and the male members of the family or anyone closely involved in the ceremony. At a wedding, once the matter of the *ilobolo* has been dealt with, praises, which are considered extremely important, are usually called out by the girl's father and her male relatives. Each line begins: 'Ziya khuleka izinkomo . . .' (The cattle are saluting . . .), filling in the name of one of the girl's male ancestors. The names that are called out go way back in time, as the men give all the praises of the male ancestors of the bride in turn. Zulu people do not consider the *ilobolo* cattle as a purchase price, but rather an honorary exchange, symbolizing the value of the bride and her ancestors. Cattle that are exchanged in this way must symbolically salute the ancestors of the new family they are entering, immortalizing their history.

After all the praises are over, the bridal party breaks into another dance routine *(umphendu),* which is the family wedding march. Moving up to the groom, they take him by the hand and place him on a beautiful marriage mat that is hand-made from much sought-after *ncema* reeds. During this ceremony *(ukwaba),* other important members of the groom's party are drawn out of the crowd and placed on similar mats. They are encouraged to lie down and given their own pillow and blanket. Sometimes gifts such as a clay pot or items related to sleeping activities are also given to them.

The women from the bride's family prepare many gifts as goodwill gestures, which are presented to the groom and his people. At this point, the peace-keeper will call for order, so that the marriage vows can be made. The groom and his best man (or men) walk slowly down to the place where the bride is standing. The bride advances a few shuffling steps towards the men, maintaining a polite and subservient countenance as a sign of respect *(hlonipha).*

At a rural Zulu wedding, traditional dress is considered superior to Western dress. Friends of the two families will often dress in a Western fashion, so as not to outshine the bridal couple and their respective families. If the bride has urban connections, she may wear a white Western wedding gown for part of the day and change into traditional Zulu attire for the main part of the proceedings. She wears a *hlonipha* veil as a sign of respect to her in-laws and carries a spear, which is a very important part of the ceremony as a symbol of her transition from single to married woman.

Women may sometimes dress in men's attire at a wedding, but this is not common. If the sister of the groom has played a significant part in bringing the couple together, she may be honoured by being allowed to wear a leopard skin, which traditionally is reserved only for the groom, for men of high status or the bride. In modern society, if a woman wears a brassière instead of going bare-breasted at a wedding, this indicates that she is either engaged or married.

At the early stages of the proceedings, the groom and his family do not dress in their traditional costumes, but rather wear smart, but fairly ordinary, Western clothes, so that the bridal party can be seen looking their best without competition. The bride's brothers and the other men in her party go to an enormous amount of trouble to dress in their finest traditional costumes. Only people directly related to, or in some way important to, the families wear traditional dress, so that they stand out in the crowd.

BELOW: *Encouraged by an enthusiastic grandmother, the groom's family puts on a grand show of dancing.*

THE VOWS

Ketiwe stands opposite Vusi with her head bowed and her eyes lowered, ready to take her vows. The 'policeman' (see page 125) turns to her and asks whether she loves Vusi. Still with her head down, she quietly answers, 'You must ask Vusi first. It is he who has brought me here.' The old man turns to Vusi, who exclaims, 'No, no, it is she who must answer first. I have paid the ilobolo.' Ketiwe keeps her head down and refuses to answer. 'Her father would not have accepted it if she did not love me,' persists Vusi. This goes on for some time before one of Vusi's elderly uncles leaps up from his place on the grass and rushes over, shouting impatiently, 'Who is this impertinent girl? Get a move on! One of you answer, so that the rest of us can enjoy the dancing!'

LEFT: Dressed in the uniform of her sisterhood, an engaged girl dances energetically. The whistle around her neck is used to spur on the other dancers.

TOP: Wearing a brassière at a wedding signifies that a woman is engaged or married, while maidens (amatshitshi) go bare-breasted.

ABOVE: One of the only occasions when a woman is allowed to wear the highly prized leopard skin is at her own wedding. In most cases, traditionalists also wear a finely crafted pleated leather skirt.

TOP: *Her face covered, the bride sits demurely in her leopard skin cloak among her trousseau, surrounded by happy revellers.*
ABOVE: *The mother of the bride celebrates successfully marrying off her daughter.*
RIGHT: *Led in procession by the senior male members of the family, the bridal party shows off their dancing skills.*

Traditional Zulu wedding vows consist of only a few simple questions. The bride is usually merely asked whether she loves and accepts the bridegroom, to which she must answer either yes or no. It may seem unlikely that a bride would say no at this stage but, because of the subservient status of married Zulu women, the bride may wish to establish right up front that she is a valued member of her own family, and that she should be treated as such by her new family. If there is even the smallest chance that she will have a difficult time with her mother-in-law or her new husband's sisters and cousins, the bride may take this opportunity to make a stand, proving to all of the assembled guests that she is no push-over. In this action, she will receive vociferous support from her own family, who will bolster her position, showing the groom's family how much they value her. This whole process can become an exceptionally competitive verbal show of wills.

The girl may ask the groom: 'Why did you come down to the river to court me if you didn't love me?' to which he will reply, 'You were just one of many whom I was courting. You sent me the betrothal beads, which meant that you wanted me.' The girl may retort, 'Then why did you perform the thanking ceremony and accept the beads if you didn't love me?' By this time, the ceremony will have turned into a mock theatre, with all the spectators involved, interrupting, calling out advice or shouting for the couple to get on with things. Some of the senior men from the groom's party may come down the hill, quite angry at the girl's arrogance. However, feeling the need to establish for once and for all that she has the support of her family, she will normally refuse to back down. Matters will finally be concluded when she states, 'He must first say he loves me. Then I will say I love him, and we can carry on.'

Although the bystanders may shout and get excited, there is no animosity between the families, as this is an accepted way of making a statement of support for the bride. Members of either one of the families will frequently sing songs at a wedding, which make openly impertinent or unpleasant claims about the bride or groom. No-one takes offence; in fact, this practice of airing dirty laundry right at the start of the marriage is almost expected by the audience. If a groom has been known as something of a philanderer, the bride's family will find out all they can about him and then sing about it at the wedding. One young woman, while her fiancé was away working as a migrant labourer to pay his *ilobolo*, was often seen standing near a water tank, which was filled twice a week by a water tanker driven by a young man from the city. The groom's family had not wanted the groom to marry the girl, because they believed she was hanging around the water tank to see the driver, and not just to collect water. This incident became part of a song which was sung at the wedding.

Once the couple have pronounced that they do in fact love each other (which, by the way, does not always involve haggling), instead of kissing as a Western couple may do, they simply shake hands. They immediately throw themselves into a competitive war dance, not against each other, but rather circling each other and dancing together. The onlookers watch the dancers, judging whose performance is more fiery and showy. The bride's group rush up to join in, shouting and ululating in a frenzy of activity.

PRAISES AND WAR CRIES

An important part of many Zulu ceremonies is the *ukugiya*, a dance to entertain the crowds during which the man who is dancing receives affirmation from his friends and relatives. He puts on a comical display or fights an imaginary foe, while his friends call out his praises, which often contain astute observations on his character. At a wedding,

the *ukugiya* is performed by the groom, after which his closest friends and relatives join in. They are followed by all the other men, from young to old. While the men dance, the married women ululate and the single and engaged girls do a stamping equivalent of the *ukugiya*, heightening the mood and winding all the men up into a frenzy of dancing. Praises *(izibongo)* recounting funny, serious or important incidents in the man's life are shouted and sung while each man is performing his *ukugiya*, each praise being unique to a specific man. The praises are intended to show that the dancer has the support of all the men present, encouraging him to greater heights in his performance.

One praise given to a particular man goes, 'You are like the antbear which digs a hole but then declines to live in it, allowing porcupines and baboons to inhabit the place after you'. This refers to the man's tendency to start a task, and not see it through, but leave it for others to complete.

ABOVE: *Zulu men of the bride's party, dressed in traditional gear and carrying their fighting sticks, arrive at a wedding.*

A praise that was given to a late *isangoma* (traditional healer), who strove to educate Zulu people about the dangers of promiscuity, goes, 'The penis cannot divine because it is not an *isangoma*'. The underlying meaning contained in this praise is that the penis cannot tell for itself whether it will be infected or infect anyone else, and as a result people should think and not just follow their desires.

A praise that was given to a young man who had a reputation for being unfaithful contained a mocking reference to the fact that his grandmother always found out about his infidelities and would call him home to admonish him: 'Zonke izindaba ziyo phelela kwaGogo' (You can two-time as much as you like but eventually grandmother will find out about everything).

Another young man, who always managed to extricate himself from awkward situations, was given a praise that went, 'You can disappear behind saplings like a cockroach and, when the sticks attempt to strike you, they strike empty spaces'. Although these praises mock the men, they are delivered in a fun, companionable way.

The young men, having *giya*'d themselves into a frenzy, move off to a different place on the hillside to start the stick-fighting. Weddings are the only official time that stick-fighting competitions take place. They are attended by a captain who keeps order among the zealous young men (*see* page 93).

When young men arrive at a wedding, or at any other stage during the ceremony that a group of men moves from one place to another, they sing and chant vigorous war cries. All the imagery contained in war cries likens the men to powerful, virile

BELOW: Stick-fighting challenges are one of the highlights of a wedding, during which the engaged girls incite the men from the sidelines.

beasts, such as bulls or lions, or, less frequently, elephants. One famous Zulu war cry goes, 'You are touching the lions, the fiery lions, the lions with fire in their mouths! Don't touch us! We will turn into fiery lions!'

THE SECOND DAY

A traditional Zulu wedding is a taxing affair: after partying throughout the previous night, and spending a large part of the current day dancing and singing, the groom's people disappear into their homes, but not to rest. They presently reappear, decked out in all their traditional finery, and take up a new position at the bottom end of the *esigcawini*, while the bride's family move to the top. The groom's family then begin their dances, singing their family anthems and wedding marches. This continues until night falls and they return home.

ABOVE: The men assemble in their regiments before marching to the place where the stick-fighting will take place. Weddings, which are attended by many people from surrounding communities, are a perfect opportunity for men to demonstrate and hone their skills.

For a second night there is no sleeping. The bride and her maids of honour are taken into a specially prepared house, where they dance the night away. The rest of her party disperses into houses around the *umuzi*. A member of the groom's party goes to the cattle byre, where the ancestors are informed that the bride has arrived in her new home and everything is satisfactory. Later on, the groom's party go back to the cattle byre where at least one of the senior members of the family performs a war dance.

Inside the houses people dance, the men perform the *ukugiya* and people play a game called *ukushaya indishi* (*see also* Women, page 118). During this game, through dares and forfeits, money, which will be given to the bride, is paid into a dish. Liquor and food is sold at enormously inflated prices which people pay without complaint, since in this way they are contributing towards the marriage.

Early in the morning on the second day, while the men are tending to their cattle, the young women go around the neighbourhood singing traditional songs about the eating of meat. Around mid-morning on this day two head of cattle, which do not form part of the *ilobolo* payment, are slaughtered at the groom's *umuzi*, one in honour of the bride, and the other in honour of the father of the bride (the latter beast is known as the *ukuncama*). Although the bride's father is entitled to take a hindquarter or any other part of the slaughtered beast home with him, in practice it is usually donated towards the feeding of the wedding guests.

The bride's father determines the manner in which the beasts are to be killed. Some insist that the sacrifice be performed traditionally – by plunging a spear through the shoulders and rib-cage straight into the heart – which requires great skill. Another method entails tying the animal to a post and, with a short dagger, cutting straight through the spinal cord of the neck. Death must be instantaneous. If for some reason the cow does not die immediately, the women instantly impose a heavy fine upon the person who is performing the sacrifice. The women have lived with the cattle and do not want them to suffer in any way.

During the second day the girls of the bride's party dance in the cattle byre. This marks the first time that the bride is allowed into her in-laws' byre, starting the process of integrating her into her husband's family, and introducing her to her new ancestors.

The father of the bride often gives his daughter a cow of her own, which is known as her 'walking stick'. This cow provides her with milk until she has been 'accepted' by her husband's ancestors, that is after the birth of her first child, when she is allowed to drink milk from her husband's family's cattle (*see* page 96). This cow also forms the basis of her own herd which will be inherited by her youngest son on her death (the father's cattle are inherited by the first-born son).

THE LAST DAY

The majority of the guests, including the bride's family and most of her friends and relatives depart on the last day of the wedding. A few close friends may remain with the bride for another night, but the following morning all the girls return to their own *imizi*, leaving the young bride with one girl who may stay on as her companion for two or three months. It is not uncommon for this girl to marry into the same household once she has come of age (*see* Women, page 115).

A hard and rocky road lies ahead of the young bride now that she is alone with her new family. She has to justify her position in the household, often having to contend with a difficult mother-in-law, and possibly also aunts and sisters. From this point on, she may never be seen in public with her head bare, but must wear a head scarf or a

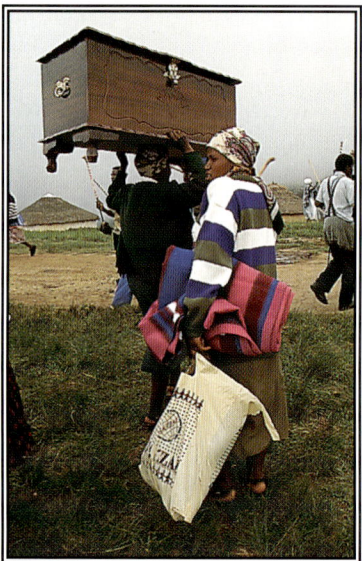

TOP: The elders and male members of the groom's family go into the cattle byre to ask the ancestors to bless the wedding.
MIDDLE: The family dance in the byre, celebrating with the ancestors.
ABOVE: The trousseau is carried to the bridal couple's new home.

head-dress *(inhloko)*, and always show politeness and deference to the male elders of the home. This *hlonipha* behaviour *(see also* pages 23 and 100) means that she should never look any of the older men in the eye, but must avert her gaze. She must never say their names directly and, if an elder, living or dead, has a name which sounds similar to an object in everyday use, out of respect for that person she may not name the item directly. A new bride frequently has to learn a whole new vocabulary of alternative words. Many people believe that, during the days when polygyny was more common, these strict rules maintained distance between a new bride and her father-in-law, who might still have been in a position to take new wives – in the past it was not unknown for a father and son to compete for the same woman.

A young bride was traditionally not allowed to drink milk, except from her own cow, or eat eggs in her new home. These taboos may seem bizarre, but they could in fact help minimize areas of friction, and protect the bride from malicious members of the family. For instance, if the chickens were not laying as well as usual, she could not be accused of stealing and eating the eggs, since she is forbidden to eat eggs. A young bride would also have to observe many taboos concerning women and cattle: when menstruating, a woman was never allowed near the cattle, because this was thought to bring bad luck to the herd and the family; women may never walk across the path of a moving herd of cattle, but have to wait for them to pass or walk behind them. These taboos are still observed today in certain traditional homes.

TOP: Traditionally the groom's female relatives jokingly try to prevent the bride from entering the groom's homestead.
ABOVE: At a wedding, the young women wear beautifully crafted beadwork skirts.

THE METAPHYSICAL WORLD

Ngeke uwakhohlise amadlozi
You cannot lie to the ancestors

Long before colonists and missionaries brought the concept of the Christian God to south-east Africa, Umvelinqangi was the all-powerful Zulu creator. Humans could not approach Umvelinqangi directly, but had to approach him through the ancestors. A number of Zulu churches today combine elements of traditional belief with Christianity.

RIGHT: *The bones are thrown! Zulu diviners (izangoma) can interpret messages from the ancestors from the way in which bones and other items thrown fall in relation to each other.*
OPPOSITE: *Khekhekhe, a famous teacher and healer (isangoma) of the Mthethwa group, has a special affinity with snakes which he uses in healing. He traces his heritage directly back to Dingiswayo, the Mthethwa king who is credited with having facilitated Shaka's rise to power.*

The ancestors, who are at the core of traditional Zulu beliefs, are referred to as *amadlozi* or *amathongo* or, in some circumstance, *izithunzi* (shadows or shades of the underworld). One of the Zulu words for sleep is *ubuthongo*, which may be derived from *amathongo*, since the ancestors are said to communicate with people in their sleep. Ancestors are not pro-active forces, but rather reactive; as such they have to be informed of any important occasion taking place in the home, such as an engagement or a coming of age ceremony. Announcements to the ancestors are usually made in the cattle byre, one of the places where the ancestors are believed to reside (*see* page 42).

Sacrifices are made to the ancestors to appeal for their assistance when things are going wrong in a person's life. Traditional healers such as *izangoma* or *izinyanga* (*see* page 142) have special powers to contact their ancestors. Usually ancestors are seen in dreams by *izangoma*, but the Zulu take numerous, usually natural, events as signs that their ancestors have re-visited a home. For instance, they do not kill the harmless snakes which may be found in the stockade of the cattle byre because they are believed to be a form of reincarnation of the ancestors.

Only a traditional healer has the power to mediate between ordinary members of society and their ancestors, which gives healers considerable influence in a community. A person with troubles will consult a diviner *(isangoma)* who, after communicating with the spirits, may tell the person that something in his life relating to the ancestors needs attention. This may be a deceased grandfather or father who has not been accorded the final rites to transport his spirit out of limbo to its final destination, which takes place some six months after the funeral. A sacrifice may be required to pacify the ancestors and restore good luck to the household. A family gathering will often be called, where there is much singing, dancing and general noise to honour the ancestors, who in certain circumstances may wish to hear jubilation and happiness in the home.

Should a family taboo, such as incest, be transgressed, the wrath of the ancestors will be invoked. If a man loses his job, someone is hurt, or a child becomes sick, it may be interpreted as the displeasure of the ancestors. When things are going badly, a Zulu person will say, 'Amadlozi angifulathele' (The ancestors have turned their backs on me, and I am left alone in this world).

As a result of their world and spiritual view which ascribes responsibility for action to an external force more powerful than themselves, Zulu people rarely see themselves in an active role. A Zulu person may say 'The car has died on me' rather than 'I did not fill the car up with petrol', or 'The bus has left me' rather than 'I missed the bus'.

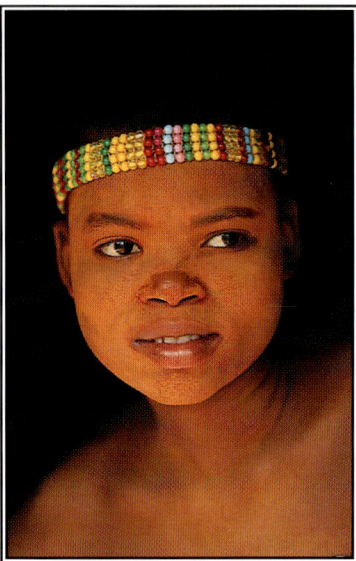

TOP: The distinctive head-dress of a traditional Zulu healer (isangoma) *with the dried goat bladder plaited into the beadwork.*

ABOVE: A trainee healer, called a thwasa *(apprentice), may be in training for as long as three years or more.*

RIGHT: Traditional healers often carry a wildebeest tail fly whisk.

OPPOSITE: Lungani Ndlovu, a cultural adviser at Simunye and a well-known isangoma, *is a light-spirited man, unlike other healers, who are usually serious.*

TRADITIONAL HEALERS

When ordinary Zulu people have minor problems, they may appeal directly to the ancestors through a small sacrificial ritual. In more serious cases, when they need to communicate with the ancestors, they believe the best way to approach them is through the mediation of a traditional healer.

A trained *isangoma* is a diviner, usually a woman, who has been specifically 'called' (*see* page 146) and trained in the methods of communicating with the ancestors. The *inyanga* on the other hand is a herbalist, who is a master of medicine with extensive

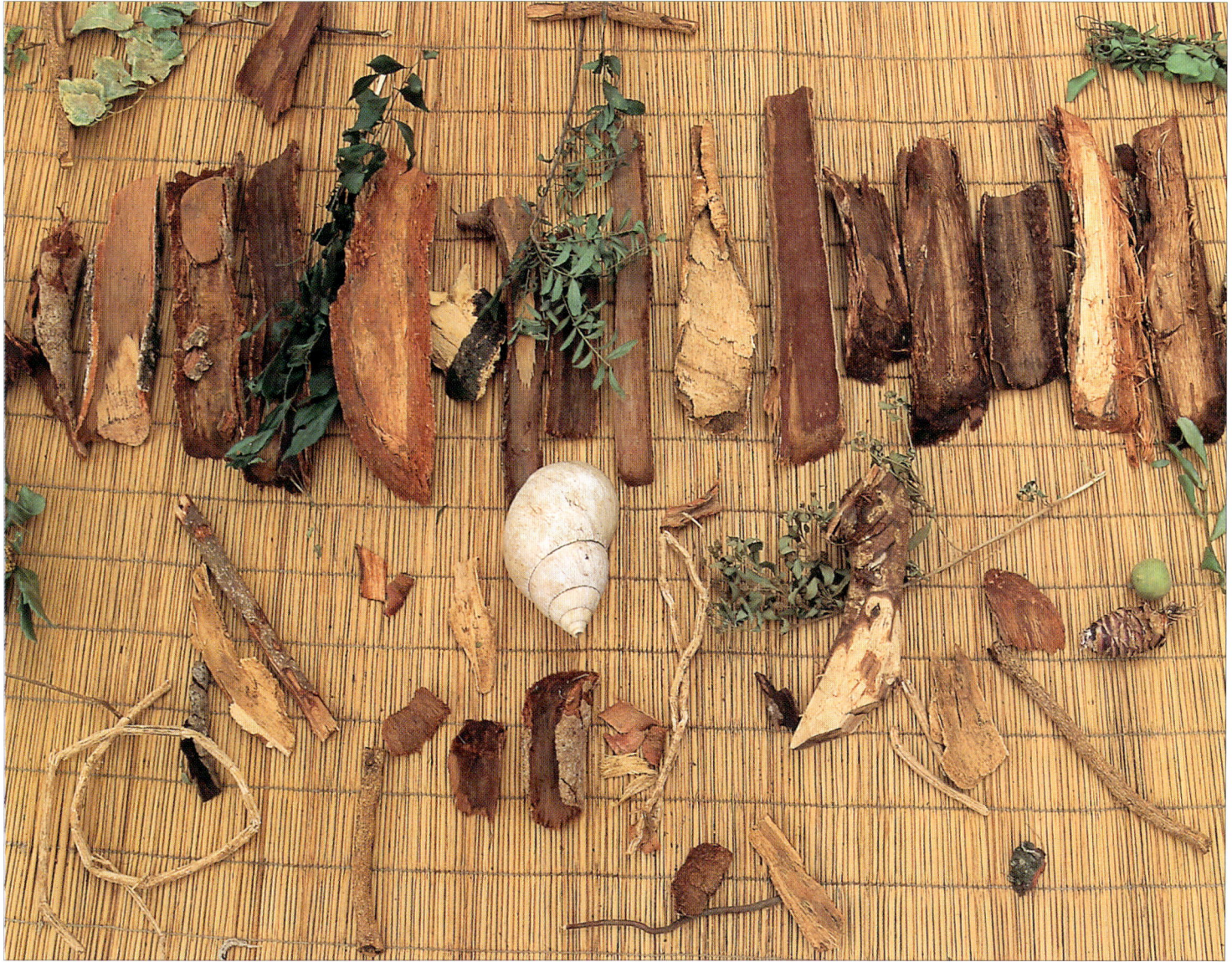

knowledge of a vast range of herbs, plants, roots and even animal products, which are used in the preparation of *umuthi* (medicine). In general, *izinyanga* are almost exclusively male, and women are discouraged from becoming herbalists. In the past, any woman who showed an interest in this field even ran the risk of being suspected of practising witchcraft.

This gender bias among the different types of Zulu healers can be attributed to a number of factors in the patriarchal society. For instance, *izinyanga* scour the country-side looking for plants and other medicinal products, and they also trade and barter plants and animal parts with fellow *izinyanga*. In traditional Zulu society, it would have been considered inappropriate for women to be wandering around the countryside on their own, or meeting with (usually male) strangers.

Despite the generally low social status accorded to Zulu women, a strong-willed woman may achieve higher standing than other women by becoming a diviner. Some males who embark upon the predominantly female diviner's apprenticeship are trained by women. They frequently adopt female dress, learn the female craft of bead-work, and also sit with the female *izangoma* on the left-hand side of a house which is traditionally reserved for women (*see* page 48). Anthropologists have surmised from

OPPOSITE: *The popular and recently deceased* inyanga, *Star Ximba, working in his consulting room, preparing medicinal potions* (umuthi) *from indigenous natural materials. Not all* izinyanga *are diviners, but they are often highly skilled herbalists who have a deep understanding of the chemical properties of plants.*
ABOVE: *Barks, herbs, roots and shells are used in preparations made by traditional healers to treat their patients.*

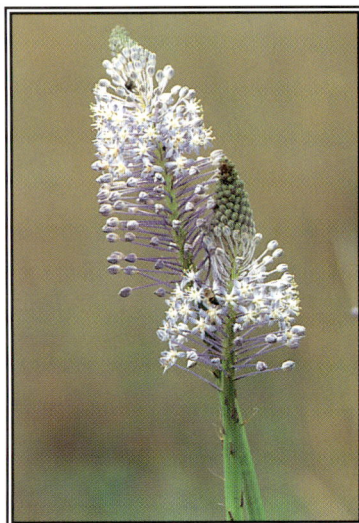

these factors that the gender bias between *izangoma* and *izinyanga* possibly provides a social role for men who, by temperament, do not necessarily fit into the overtly masculine Zulu mould. However, the incidence of cross-dressing is not limited to male *izangoma* – women may be seen wearing men's clothing at weddings or in celebrations for the Heavenly Princess, Nomkhubulwana.

A third type of traditional diviner is the *umthakathi* (sorcerer) but, as this sect is relatively secretive and is seldom spoken of in open conversation, little is known about their practices. *Abathandazi* are prophets who are associated with the various independent church movements, and their healing is generally done through prayer and sanctification by holy water and ash, rather than through the ancestors or recourse to plant or animal remedies.

Apart from having access to the ancestors that is denied to the ordinary people, Zulu healers treat illnesses ranging from physical to psychological and spiritual. An *inyanga*'s training tends to focus on treating ailments by means of plants and animal products, while the *isangoma* is typically guided by her ancestors towards the remedies required. However, since the Zulu frequently do not separate physical from mental or spiritual ailments, healers of all types need to have some knowledge of both the metaphysical world and plant lore.

TRAINING FOR
TRADITIONAL HEALERS

In Zulu culture, a person does not simply choose to be a healer. Instead healers, particularly diviners, are 'called' to their profession by their ancestors, often in a dream. A person who has been called may become ill, show mental disturbance or experience emotional turmoil. This is not congenital madness or ordinary mental instability, although it may be obvious that the person is going through tremendous psychological upheaval. The person may also experience recurring dreams, bouts of sneezing, spells of dizziness, and even periods of unconsciousness. All of this will indicate that the ancestors are calling and must be obeyed.

The path to becoming a traditional healer is considered harsh in Zulu society. On first receiving a sign from their ancestors, many people appeal to the ancestors, by sacrificing a goat, to release them from the calling. However, if the ancestors do not relieve the person of the malady, the only option is to obey the calling by going into an apprenticeship. The person who has been called will sometimes feel an urge to travel to distant places and will walk for several days, often not knowing where he or she is going. The destination more often than not turns out to be the home of a senior *isangoma* or instructor. The apprentice *(thwasa)* will live with the mentor for at least six months, serving the *isangoma* and receiving instruction from her. Finally the time will come when it is apparent that the apprentice has become sufficiently proficient. Along with other apprentices, the *thwasa* will be tested at a 'coming out' or graduation ceremony. The *thwasa* may have to discover hidden items, and the length of time it takes to find them indicates the strength of the links to the ancestors.

Like Western practitioners, *izangoma* need to develop a reputation in their community. Those who are perceived to have strong powers and connections to their ancestors may become enormously influential. However, not all apprentices become successful practising diviners, many falling by the wayside, eventually returning to their former lives. These people are considered *phupha*'d which means they 'can only dream, and can no longer talk of reality'.

PLANTS AND ANIMALS IN HEALING

A strong link exists between the ancestors and the natural kingdom. For centuries, traditional healers have been using indigenous plants and animals, not just as food or for decorative reasons, but also for medicinal purposes and divining. The use of animals in traditional healing practices is often more symbolic than biochemical. Ingredients for *umuthi* (medicine), whether plant or animal, are usually used in conjunction with other products to make potions, which are administered in a number of ways. Depending on the application, a patient may be required to wear an amulet, part of the potion may be burned around the homestead or sprinkled in special places.

ABOVE: Before working with the ancestors, an isangoma and his or her initiates clear their senses with a special plant, usually impepho.

FOLLOWING PAGES: Khekhekhe, the famous Mthethwa snake man, holds up a puffadder during a ceremony.

TOP: An isangoma's *necklace made from items such as bones, teeth and feathers.*
ABOVE: Details of an isangoma's *fly whisk and cowrie belt. Great secrecy surrounds these healers, but the articles depicted in both pictures above are believed to endow the* isangoma *with magical potency.*

The medication may be administered to the body by drinking or rubbing on the skin. It may also be introduced into the body through incisions, which are normally made to the ankles, wrists, chest and waist.

A small portion of an animal or bird that represents characteristics the Zulu admire may be included in *umuthi*. For example, the ground hornbill (*Bucorvus leadbeateri*), which is known in Zulu as *intsingizi* or *ingududu*, walks slowly and deliberately through the grasslands looking for food. Its calm, dignified air is admired by the Zulu, and the ground hornbill is in great demand in *umuthi* preparations. If part of an eagle is used in a medicinal application, the drinker is believed to imbibe the bird's strength and majesty. Another popular mixture is made from ground swallow bones, herbs and plants, mixed with hippo fat into a gritty paste, which is burned at the same time every day for a few weeks in the centre of the cattle byre. This application is purported to 'teach' the cattle to come home at the same time every day. It is possible that the smell of burning herbs attracts the cattle. Traditional healers, however, maintain that the swallow bones are the powerful ingredient in the paste, since swallows go far from home, but always return at the same time every year.

A potion containing the powdered bones of the ground hornbill is rubbed into incisions on the shoulder blades to prevent the person from being struck by lightning. The hamerkop (*Scopus umbretta*), or *uthekwane* in Zulu, may frequently be spotted in pairs; because of this characteristic, healers use them to make a medicine to 'hold a husband's heart', in other words, to keep him faithful.

Night birds are often connected to evil, and parts of the barn owl are used in the casting and countering of many spells. The Zulu take their superstition about owls so seriously that they frequently put spikes onto the apex of their homes to prevent owls from settling on the roof and casting spells on the household. Healers need to know how and when to use a certain application. Alive, owls may be harbingers of bad news or evil spirits, but dead they can be used to help people with little energy who feel sleepy during the day.

Recently there has been an outcry from animal activists about the supply of certain animals and plants to the traditional healing trade. Unemployment has driven many unqualified people into the countryside in search of ingredients to supply the needs of the many urban healers. Through such practices, many plants are harvested to the point of extinction and some animals are being placed on the endangered list. Before the introduction of fenced game reserves, the Zulu and their traditional healers had access to a greater variety of game than they do today. Previously, taboos and restrictions were imposed on hunting or killing certain animals, particularly royal game such as elephant and leopard. Despite this, healers had far greater access to many of the larger game species than they have today. Because of the difficulties involved in obtaining healing materials, healers have learnt to substitute animals: many of the larger birds (eagles, vultures, ground hornbill and ostrich) are now used instead of mammals such as wildebeest, buffalo and rhino.

Healers have also developed their own individual applications, which may differ from healer to healer and from region to region. Some believe that a monkey should never be dismembered but should be sold whole, while others will buy just a small piece. Monkeys are often used to prevent miscarriages, because Zulu healers say that monkeys seldom miscarry. Whether whole or in pieces, almost all the parts of an animal are used by healers to treat their patients. In the case of birds, feathers and even the shell and the contents of the egg may be used on the rare occasions they are available, although many healers prefer not to use either eggs or small chicks because they believe that the *umuthi* is not yet strong.

TABOOS RELATING TO HARVESTING

During the years of apartheid rule in South Africa, it became extremely difficult for traditional healers to obtain the indigenous products they required to prepare the *umuthi* needed to treat their patients, as game reserves were fenced off and harvesting of indigenous products was prohibited by law. As they no longer had direct access to the resources, in many cases they resorted to buying animals and plants which were poached, or brought in illegally from neighbouring countries by untrained collectors. While more conservative traditional healers still observe the harvesting ethics from the past, urbanization and the reliance on untrained collectors mean that many of the old beliefs and practices are falling away.

BELOW: Healers (izangoma) dance themselves into a trance in the cattle byre, where they are close to their ancestors.

In historical times, certain rituals had to be observed when an animal was killed or a plant was removed from the soil. For instance, the minute that a sacrificed wildebeest fell to the ground, a healer would tie a small knot in its tail hair to 'prevent the power of the spirit escaping'. The python *(inhlwathi)* is an animal that is closely associated with the ancestors. Whenever an *inhlwathi* was killed, a white goat would be sacrificed, as a supplication to the ancestors to restore the healing qualities of the python. These days, if a healer kills an *ufudu* (tortoise) for medicinal purposes, a small piece of white bread, which is an item of luck, should be inserted into the mouth of the tortoise, to ensure that the medicine that is made from it is good.

All plants and animals, in fact all living things, were believed to contain certain power *(amandla)*, but the power of plants was generally neutral, and a plant could be used for either good or evil. Today plants growing in the wild are considered to have far greater powers than cultivated plants. Forests are places of great power and magic, where the most potent medicinal plants may be found; the older the forest, the stronger the medicinal powers of the plants in it, and the older the trees the more potent the bark taken from it. In the Zulu kingdom, kings were frequently buried in ancient forests.

Many people avoid these forests, believing that they are inhabited by dwarf-sized tongue-tied zombies *(imikhovu)*, who are often associated with witches. Many harmful plants used by sorcerers are also found deep in these forests.

In the old days, a person who pointed at another was thought to be a wizard, and a man who let his shadow fall on the shadow of another was believed to be draining his life-essence. It is extremely unlucky to point an index finger at a medicinal plant or to allow one's shadow to fall across it, as both these actions are believed to damage the plant. More conservative healers will thus always try to collect plants which have never been 'over-shadowed' by a human being. Water collected from a crevice in a cave is said to have more healing powers than water from a tap, because no person could jump over a cave and cast his shadow over it.

Certain medicinal plants may be collected only if the collector is wearing traditional attire or is naked, while others must be collected at full moon. The bark of *nukani* or stinkwood *(Ocotea bullata)* is thought to obtain magical or medicinal powers only once the wound of the scarred tree has healed. Anthropologist Frans Prins explains that 'a collector should always address the medicinal plants by their Zulu names when removing them and should ask their permission to do so. Ideally the collector should tell the plant what he or she intends doing with it'. The plant should be treated with the same respect as the ancestors, and money or a piece of white bread, should be put in the hole left when the plant is removed to bring good luck. Some healers place a piece of their hair on the spot, 'to replace the power which has been removed from the soil', as recorded by Frans Prins.

People who are 'polluted' in any way should not handle medicinal plants because they will diminish the power of the plant. People who are considered polluted include those who have returned from a funeral, a woman who has recently given birth or is menstruating, a person who had sexual intercourse the day before, a woman who has had an abortion and men returning from battle.

KHEKHEKHE

The mists shift over the damp grass; through the half light and the dripping leaves, an apparition appears, but is quickly swallowed by the swirls of low cloud. An enigmatic male figure can finally be distinguished. Khekhekhe the healer stands on the path, draped in four enormous snakes.

Khekhekhe, one of the most formidable and prominent *izangoma* in the northern KwaZulu-Natal region, can trace his lineage back to Dingiswayo, Shaka's mentor. Khekhekhe and his snakes are often called upon for rituals and dances prior to important events. The Zulu believe that all the secrets of man's behaviour can be found in nature; to Khekhekhe snakes demonstrate man's closeness to nature and he uses them as his medium of healing. When he needs to collect snakes, he will often strip himself naked and, dressed only in grass, he will venture into the wilderness. He releases his snakes from time to time and, instead of going out to look for new snakes, he may appeal to his ancestors. Shortly after this, snakes mysteriously find their way into an empty house that he has set aside for them. He believes it is his affinity with creation that makes his snakes return to him and in fact enjoy being with him.

Khekhekhe is also a prominent teacher who at any time will be accompanied by a number of *thwasas*. He has seven wives, six of whom are three sets of sisters. He claims it is always much easier to marry sisters, because they squabble much less.

BELOW: Urban healers obtain the plants and animals they need in preparing umuthi *from street traders in the busy urban centres. Ordinary Zulu people will also frequent these traders.*
BOTTOM: Bottles of potions fill a healer's consulting room.

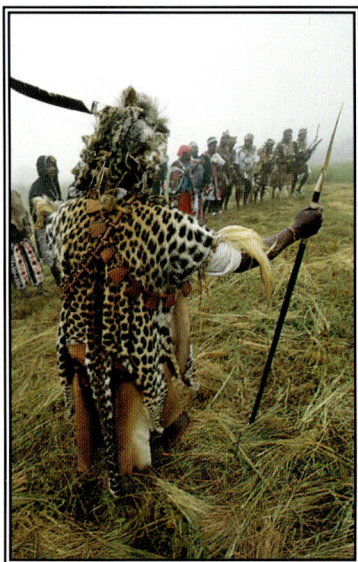

TRADITIONAL HEALING TODAY

As a member of an executive team, Bongani was flown to Cape Town by his employers to attend a conference. Much excitement preceded this, his first ever flight, but, at the end of the conference, when the time came for him to return home, he refused to fly, and other travel arrangements had to be made. As well as being a senior executive, Bongani is also a prominent traditional healer in northern KwaZulu-Natal. He explained that, when he was in the air, he felt cut off from his guiding ancestral spirits, which made him feel uncomfortable and vulnerable. He vowed not to place himself in such a situation again.

Early settlers and missionaries dismissed traditional healers as 'quacks' or evil 'witch-doctors' and many people believed that, with the introduction of Western medicine, traditional healing would disappear. However, traditional healing has been in existence for hundreds of years and is still very popular. In fact, the role of traditional healers has recently been recognized by South Africa's Medical and Dental Council.

The Zulu people maintain that Western medicine does not address the full spectrum of illnesses, mental and physical, which afflict humans. They believe that some diseases are of African origin which cannot be understood or treated by a Western practitioner. In traditional healing, it is important to heal the mind as well as the physical body. Recent studies indicate that many urban Zulu people consult Western doctors and attend clinics when they are suffering from a serious physical ailment, but they also continue to consult their traditional healers. With the increase in urbanization and the resultant lack of housing and jobs, Zulu people are increasingly consulting traditional healers who they feel are better equipped to help in these stressful circumstances.

AFRICAN VERSIONS OF CHRISTIANITY

Early missionaries tolerated no deviation from their version of Christianity and strongly disapproved of any traditional practices. Zulu converts were expected to turn their backs on their culture. This included changing the way they dressed since, in the minds of the missionaries, animal skins were closely associated with paganism.

Over the years, Zionism has emerged as the most popular religion in South Africa. While it adheres to many of the basic tenets of Christianity and the Old Testament, it

OPPOSITE, TOP AND BOTTOM: Khekhekhe leads his graduates at their graduation ceremony. The man standing behind him in the top picture is his son, who is also an isangoma.
***BELOW:** Apprentices dance at a graduation ceremony for healers.*

THE MESSENGER HOLY APOSTOLIC
BISHOP
M.M. SIKAKANE
CHURCH IN ZION S.A.

OPPOSITE: The Bishop M. M. Sikakane of the Zionist Church in Njomelwane near Melmoth in KwaZulu-Natal.
LEFT: Zionists, dressed in their distinctive white outfits, gather to pray in their little corrugated iron church.
ABOVE AND TOP: A mission chapel and bell tower situated near Eshowe in the heart of KwaZulu-Natal.

does make exceptions, for instance polygyny which is still tolerated in certain sects. Some sociologists partly ascribe the proliferation of the Zionist church to apartheid: the church was one of the very few places in which the Zulu, or any other African people, could rise to positions of leadership.

From the very early days there was a divide between Christian converts (*amakholwa*) and Zulu traditionalists (*amabhinca* or 'those who wear something wrapped around them'). Before, during and even after the Anglo-Zulu war of 1879 (*see* page 34), there

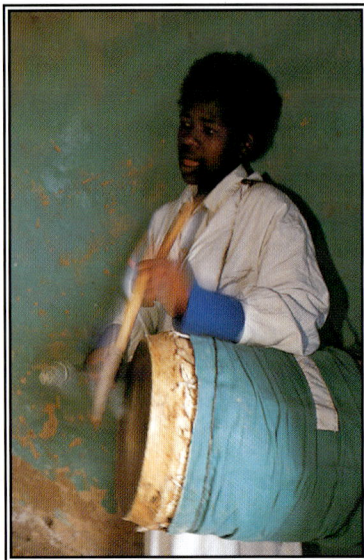

TOP LEFT: *Zionist worshippers*
on their way to church.
ABOVE: *Traditional Zulu drums*
play a significant part in Zionist
church meetings.
TOP RIGHT: *Zionists gather to*
pray during a church service.

were a few minor purges by the *amabhinca* of Christians who were seen to be siding with, and thus aiding, the British Imperial forces which were defeating the Zulu kingdom and threatening the old traditional order.

The divide between the *amakholwa* and the *amabhinca* has, in many ways, persisted to modern times, but there are also many instances where traditional culture has been incorporated into Western, Christian practices, and conversely where Christianity has influenced traditional Zulu activities. It is not unusual to attend a wedding in a very traditional rural setting, where the groom will be attired in traditional regalia, wearing leopard and other animal skins, supported by all his men, also dressed in traditional clothing carrying their shields and fighting sticks, but the bride will appear attired in a white Western-style wedding gown and be attended by her bridesmaids, all dressed in satin and carrying flowers.

In a similar way, Zulu Christians may consult an *abathandazi* (commonly known as an *umpolofiti*, derived from prophet) who can see into the future like an Old Testament prophet. They may also visit an *isangoma* or an *inyanga*, or make a sacrifice to their ancestors, when they are afflicted with an illness that is African in origin and which must be treated in a traditional manner. Other diseases, which are Western, need to be treated by Western medicine.

The *Ibandla lamaNazaretha*, which was founded by Isaiah Shembe in 1911 and is known colloquially as the Shembe Church, has taken the cultural context further than the Zionists, in that they make a point of wearing traditional costumes for their religious ceremonies. In addition, they have incorporated movement and dance into their observances. Despite being polygynous, members of the *Ibandla lamaNazaretha* have very strict moral codes of conduct, and abstain from drinking alcohol and smoking, and on Saturday, their Sabbath, they may only eat cold food. Members of the *Ibandla lamaNazaretha* worship on Saturdays rather than Sundays, because many of their teachings are based on the Old Testament.

DEATH

When Zulu people die, according to tradition, their bodies must be returned to their ancestral home so that their soul can be at peace (failure to do this could lead to a problematic ancestor). The family will go to great lengths to ensure that, if for some reason the actual body cannot be returned, the spirit is still 'fetched' home. They do this with a branch from the buffalo thorn tree (*umlahlankosi*), which is believed to have the power to 'contain' and transport the spirits of the deceased from afar. It is not unusual to see a Zulu person travelling on a bus, train or taxi, carrying a buffalo thorn tree branch. A man bringing the spirit of a deceased member of his family home may not speak to anyone in transit, lest the spirit feels abandoned and flies off. Two tickets must be purchased on any transport vehicle, one for the living, and one for the dead, to ensure that the spirit is not left behind.

When the head of a household dies, he is buried inside the cattle byre (*see* page 42), but any other members of the family will generally be buried in an area outside the stockade of the *umuzi*. The night before the funeral, family members from all around the country will arrive, and the body will be placed inside the home. Candles are lit, and an all-night vigil is kept. If the deceased died unnaturally, such as in an accident or in violent circumstances, the body is not brought into the home to prevent the bad luck that struck the deceased from entering with it. Instead a small grass or, these days, canvas shelter is built outside the *umuzi* and the vigil is held there.

The Zulu have a highly developed concept of pollution which is connected to darkness (*umnyama*), and is often associated with birth or death. Washing is one of the ways, both physical and symbolic, to cleanse oneself of *isinyama*. On returning home from a funeral, people are required to wash their hands in the contents of a goat's stomach mixed with water *umswani* in order to cleanse themselves of the blackness of death. If the person died in unnatural circumstances, the vehicle in which the body was transported also has to be sprinkled with the purifying liquid. These days, a small bowl of soap and water may suffice.

BOTTOM LEFT: A community procession follows a Zulu chief's funeral.
BELOW: A sprig from umlahlankosi, *the buffalo thorn tree* (Ziziphus mucronata), *which is used to 'bring home' the spirit of a person who dies away from home, even if for some reason his body has to be left behind.*

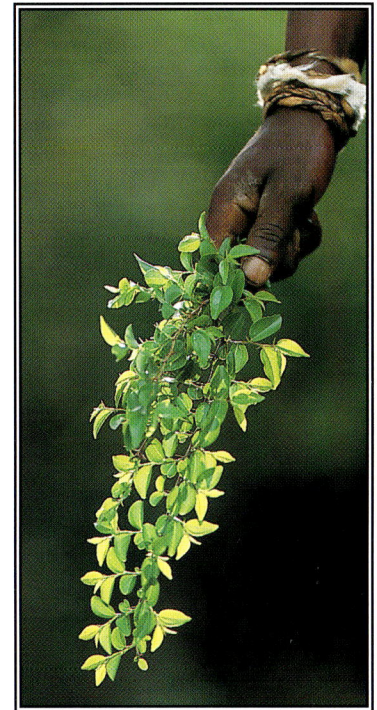

GLOSSARY

A

ABATHANDAZI

Normally Zionist Christians, these are **healers** who can see problems through visions. They treat people through a combination of prayer, the application of holy water and laying on of hands.

AMADLOZI

At the core of Zulu beliefs are the **ancestors**, deceased members of a family who can intervene in the spirit world on behalf of the living. The ancestors need to be acknowledged, appeased and kept informed of any changes or special events that are taking place in the family or the community. Traditional healers, such as *izangoma*, have the power to contact the ancestors, which they may do through dreams. Sacrifices are made to the ancestors in the cattle byre, where they are believed to reside.

AMAGALIGA

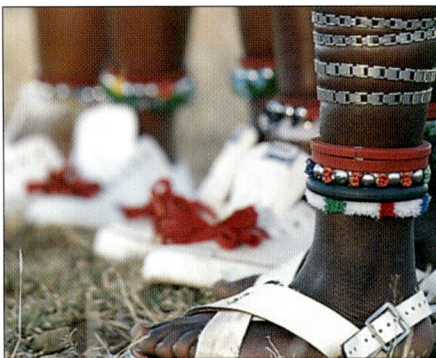

Young Zulu women wear beautifully **beaded anklets** for special occasions such as marriages and coming of age ceremonies. Rattles may be attached to the anklets, which the girls shake while they are dancing.

AMANTOMBAZANE

This word, which literally means **'little girls'**, is a generic term used for young unmarried females.

AMAQHIKIZA

Engaged girls are allowed far more freedom than is usually enjoyed by women in traditional Zulu society. Normally the man to whom an engaged girl is betrothed is paying a high bride wealth (*ilobolo*), but it has not yet been fully paid to her father. She has a measure of autonomy, since she is considered no longer under the control of her father, nor is she yet obliged to comply with the rules of her husband. At weddings engaged girls may be seen dancing with wild abandon, using a short fighting stick. They behave in an Amazonian way, and are generally rebellious.

AMASHINGA

Mavericks, men who thrive on stick-fighting, can be likened to gun slingers in the wild west. They will go to great lengths to seek out other well-known stick-fighters. By defeating them they enhance their own reputations even more.

AMASI

Curdled milk is cultured by taking fresh milk out of the *ithunga* (milking pail) directly into a milk gourd where it turns to *maas* or *amasi*. The grandmother of the home is in charge of dispensing the *amasi*.

AMATSHITSHI

A **maiden** who has not yet chosen her husband walks around bare-breasted, with her head uncovered, as a sign of her marital status.

H

HLONIPHA

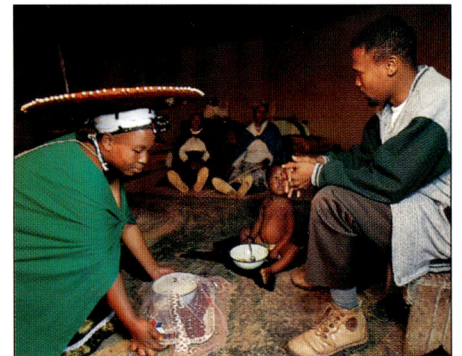

Although **respect** is shown by people of both sexes, in the context of this book *hlonipha* has been used to denote the specific form in which women defer to men and accord them status. *Hlonipha* is demonstrated by various forms of body language and protocol, for instance when a woman serves a man she should ensure that her head is never on a higher level than his.

I

IBANDLA

The **council** is a important part of Zulu society, where the men meet to discuss the issues that affect the whole community. No matters are too small or too great to be discussed here, and this communal decision-making by means of group consensus is the backbone of Zulu authority.

ICECE

A girl's **coming of age** is an important ceremony, when a father honours his daughter for having guarded her good name. He acknowledges that she is now ready to look for a suitor and get married. An animal is slaughtered and an entire afternoon is spent in dancing. Money is pinned to a scarf which she wears while dancing. Prior to the actual coming of age the girl spends several months in seclusion, being coached in the ways of womanhood, and treated as a lady of leisure.

IKHOHLO

In a polygynous household, the **left-hand wife** lives in the 'smaller' or 'lesser' part of the *umuzi*, the right-hand part being the 'greater' part.

IKLWA

The broad-bladed, short-handled **stabbing spear** which was introduced by King Shaka.

ILALA NYATHI

The **sleeping buffalo tree** is a wood favoured specifically for the making of fighting sticks.

ILOBOLO

When a man wishes to marry, he will send emissaries to the father of the girl, to negotiate the **bride wealth**, which needs to be paid before the actual marriage can take place.

INDUNA

A **headman** is appointed by the chief because he has popular support. His function is to resolve petty cases, and those that are too complicated he will refer to the chief. The headman represents the chief within his specific *isigodi* (geographic community).

INKOSI

The **chief** of a lineage, who in the past owed allegiance directly to the king.

INKOSIKAZI

An important man, such as a chief, usually has a **great wife** who is of royal blood. If he has more than one wife, the great wife will not necessarily be his first wife but will be chosen in consultation with the elders. Her first son is the most important son in the *umuzi*, who inherits his father's cattle.

INYONI KAYIPHUMULI

The **royal Zulu herd** of white Nguni cattle with distinctive black or red ears. In Shaka's time, they were so numerous that the oxpeckers never rested, going from beast to beast, which is how they came to be known as 'the bird never rests'.

IPASI

This beaded **choker chain** is given by a girl to her lover as part of the build-up towards marriage.

ISIJULA

This small-headed **throwing spear** is used for hunting antelope, because it travels a great distance. It is also used for sacrifices as it leaves a very small hole in the hide.

ISISILA SENKONJANE

Traditionally the **swallow-tailed battle axe** that was carried by royalty and used to control their warriors during battle.

ISITHEBE

These **mats**, woven from durable material, are used by women when grinding food on a stone.

ISITROBHO

Borrowed from the Afrikaans word *strop*, this is the **leather thong** that goes around an ox's neck to keep it in the yoke. Symbolically this is also worn by a young girl to show that she still has control of herself and no-one as yet has put her in the yoke because she does not have a boyfriend.

ISIXANU

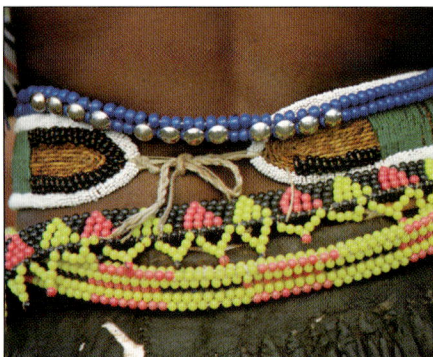

After giving birth, a woman wears a **maternity belt** to flatten her stomach. (*See also* **IZINKOMO ZESIXANU**.)

ISIZENZE

The **battle axe** that is generally employed by commoners to push, grab and gash.

IZINKOMO ZESIXANU

When a woman marries, her father may give her some cattle of her own, which are known as the **cattle of the maternity belt**. These form the basis of her own herd, which are separate from those owned by her husband. As a young bride in her new home, she is not allowed to drink milk from the cows of her husband's herd until she has produced a baby, but she may drink milk from her own cows. The cattle of the maternity belt is inherited by her last-born son on her death.

IZINDLU

The traditional **'beehive' house**, made from saplings and grass, is still seen in parts of rural KwaZulu-Natal. These days bricks and other more durable material are often used.

IZIQU

These **medallions of war**, made from various hard woods, are worn as a kind of bandoleer over the shoulder. If a man defeats another at war, the loser's medallions would be taken from him and worn by the other as a sign of his victory.

M

MPONDO ZANKOMO

The very early time in the morning is known as **the horns of the cattle**. As the day starts to dawn, it is possible to make out the silhouettes of the horns of the cattle in the cattle byre.

T

THEMBA

Beaded squares are given by young women to men to wear around their necks. A *Themba* is a promise that his attentions to that girl are not in vain – he might in fact be the one she finally chooses as a husband.

U

UBUSENGA

These **leggings** are made from cattle or horse hair. Long bits are taken from the tail and wire is wound around this to form a tight bangle.

UCU

When a girl accepts a man as her husband, she will give him **betrothal beads**, which are generally white, although other symbolic colours such as blue and red may also be included. They are threaded around a man's neck with one long piece hanging down to his waist. These beautiful beads signal to all the world that his suit has been successful.

UKUCIMELA

Before a bride-to-be sets off from her father's *umuzi* to that of her fiancé's parents for her wedding, she goes to all her relatives and requests farewell **presents** from each of them.

UKUGIYA

A symbolic **dance-fight** against an imaginary opponent, the *ukugiya* is a display of masculine personal prowess, which is laced with humour to amuse the crowd. This is part of the way that Zulu people entertain each other in the build-up to any important ceremony or occasion such as a wedding. The *ukugiya* is also used as a preparation for battle when men are in dead earnest about a fight; all the humour drops away and it is used as a means of inciting the warriors for battle.

UKUGQUBUSHELA

A **competitive dance** between the families of the bride and groom, this sets the tone of fun and games for the whole wedding, making the two parties very competitive against one another.

UMBALA OMNYAMA

The **royal herd of Swazi cattle** are traditionally black.

UMLAHLANKOSI

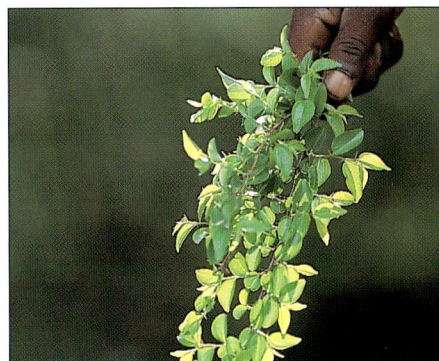

Should a man die far from home and for some reason it is not possible to transport his body back home, a member of his family or a friend will take a branch of the **buffalo thorn tree** to the place where he has died. The spirit is asked to enter into the branch, which is used to transport the spirit back to the deceased person's home.

UMNUMZANE

A Zulu man is the **undisputed head of his household**, who has the final say in all important matters.

UMPHENDU

One of the key **dances** at a wedding, this is performed for members of a specific lineage when they marry.

UMTHAKATHI

A very anti-social **sorceror**, the *umthakathi* uses black magic in order to bring bad luck to other people.

UMUTHI

Traditional medicine, unless it is made from animal products, is generally made from trees and herbs. For this reason, the word *umuthi* is derived comes from the Zulu word for 'tree'

UMUZI

An **extended homestead** generally has a single founder, a married man, who lives there with his wife or wives and all of their children. Traditionally, once the father of the home dies and a respectful time has elapsed, the rest of the family will move from that spot, leaving him in peace. They would then go off to start their own homestead. Now that more permanent building materials are used, this practice is falling away.

INDEX

Page numbers in **bold** refer to illustrations